GLYN REES is a writer, illustrator, book designer and cartoonist with numerous publications to his credit. His work has appeared in *Punch* and many other national newspapers and magazines. He loves all kinds of humorous verse, from Ewart to Spilligan, but is particularly fond of that peculiar, yet enduring, British institution – the limerick!

GRAY JOLLIFFE has been a cartoonist and illustrator ever since people started paying him to do it. He also had a career in advertising as a copywriter and creative director in some of London's top agencies. Since then he has scratched a living illustrating several books, notably *Man's Best Friend* with Peter Mayle (an old advertising friend), *The Unadulterated Cat* with Terry Pratchett and his own book *Apathy Made Easy*.

As well as cartoons and animations for advertising, he appears in a variety of magazines and newspapers and has a regular cartoon strip called Chloe and Co. in the *Daily Mail*. Predominantly a writer, his cartoons start with the words to which he adds a drawing if he can think of one.

Also available

THE MAMMOTH BOOK OF
FILTHY LIMERICKS

EDITED BY GLYN REES

ILLUSTRATED BY GRAY JOLLIFFE

ROBINSON

RUNNING PRESS
PHILADELPHIA · LONDON

Constable & Robinson Ltd
3 The Lanchesters
162 Fulham Palace Road
London W6 9ER
www.constablerobinson.com

First published in the UK by Robinson,
an imprint of Constable & Robinson Ltd, 2009

A copy of the British Library Cataloguing in Publication
Data is available from the British Library

UK ISBN 978-1-84529-682-7

1 3 5 7 9 10 8 6 4 2

First published in the United States in 2009 by Running Press Book Publishers.

9 8 7 6 5 4 3 2 1
Digit on the right indicates the number of this printing

US Library of Congress number: 2008944137
US ISBN 978-0-7624-3730-6

Running Press Book Publishers
2300 Chestnut Street
Philadelphia, PA 19103-4371

Visit us on the web!
www.runningpress.com

Illustrated by Gray Jolliffe

Designed by Mitchell Associates
www.mitch.uk.com

Printed and bound in the EU

CONTENTS

INTRODUCTION

Be honest – if pushed, you could just about remember, and recite, a couple of filthy or bawdy limericks, or fragments of limericks. We all can. The mind is an amazing organ – other amazing organs are mentioned elsewhere in this book – that, in no time at all, dredges up all kinds of recollections of the fantastic attributes and/or astounding achievements of an array of interesting and unusual characters: a certain young girl from Devizes, the constable whose appendage had sadly long ceased to properly function, or that particularly fortunate motorcyclist from Horton…

It's not surprising that the most enduring verse form in the English language has established itself so deeply in our popular culture. It has, after all, been around for a long, long time. The first examples may have been composed circa 400BC by the Ancient Greeks. We all know what dirty buggers they were; and their greatest comic poet, Aristophanes, did have a reputation as a bit of a lad!

The word "bawd", incidentally, is an old word for a brothel keeper. It comes from a French word "baud", meaning merry or lively. Bawdy stories therefore, are the sort that contain lighthearted reference to sexual activities, such as might be associated with brothels, hence: bawdy limericks!

Many believe that a gentleman named Edward Lear invented the modern limerick. He didn't, though he unquestionably helped to popularize the form in his *Book of Nonsense*, published initially in 1846, and reprinted in 1863. Being Drawing Master to Queen Victoria and her children, Lear would not have wanted to upset his employer unduly. As a result, his verses were of a fairly innocuous nature, though they were soon being parodied by others, so that

There was a Young Lady from Norway
Who casually sat in a doorway;
  When the door squeezed her flat,
  She exclaimed: "What of that?"
This courageous Young Lady of Norway.

very quickly became:

> There was a Young Lady from Norway
> Who hung by her toes in a doorway;
>   She said to her beau:
>   "Just look at me, Joe,
>   I think I've discovered one more way!"

probably at the hands of the mischievous Algernon Charles Swinburne (1837–1909), a well-known poet and contemporary of Alfred Lord Tennyson, also reputed to have written a handful of bawdy limericks.

Swinburne was born and lived in London during the Victorian era. Considered a decadent poet, he was, by all accounts, an excitable character who drank heavily. Although his reputation was of a man who derived pleasure from sado-masochistic sexual pursuits, he may have talked about such exploits more than he actually indulged in them. Oscar Wilde famously insisted that Swinburne was "a braggart in matters of vice, who had done everything he could to convince his fellow citizens of his homosexuality and bestiality without being in the slightest degree a homosexual or a bestializer".

Braggart or not, when he died at the age of seventy-two, following a mental and physical breakdown, Swinburne's mastery of vocabulary, rhyme and metre had placed him amongst the most talented English language poets in history.

Here are a couple more of his clever Lear parodies:

There was an old man of Cape Horn,
Who wished he had never been born;
  So he sat on a chair,
  Till he died of despair,
That dolorous man of Cape Horn

> There was a young man of Cape Horn,
> Who wished he had never been born;
>   And he wouldn't have been
>   If his father had seen
> That the end of the rubber was torn.

There was an old man of Dundee,
Who frequented the top of a tree;
  When disturbed by the crows,
  He abruptly arose,
And exclaimed: "I'll return to Dundee."

> There was an old man of Dundee,
> Who molested an ape in a tree:
>   The result was most horrid,
>   All arse and no forehead,
> Three balls and a purple goatee.

This may have been the beginning of the indecent (or filthy) limerick, although it is more likely that the clean and indecent varieties had existed side by side for some time. Perhaps, in the same way that Lear popularized the one kind, Swinburne and his friends popularized the other. Both can be equally entertaining and are perfectly acceptable nowadays, provided that they are well-constructed, clever and, most importantly of all – funny!

Although the playwright Arnold Bennett clearly thought otherwise when he declared: "All I have to say about limericks is that the best ones are entirely unprintable", a classic "limerick limerick" neatly sums up the pro-bawdy hypothesis:

It needn't have ribaldry's taint,
Or strive to make everyone faint;
   There's a type that's demure
   And perfectly pure,
Though it helps quite a lot if it ain't!

Arthur Wimperis, who wrote so many great British musical comedies, added: "The only limericks in my experience of any literary merit are distinctly Rabelaisian. Beside these, the more polite and printable examples fade away into the dim haze of mediocrity."

Don Marquis, another humorist, from across the Atlantic, divided limericks into three distinct types: "Limericks to be told when ladies are present; limericks to be told when ladies are absent, but clergymen are present – and LIMERICKS!"

Louis Untermeyer, a New Yorker who not only wrote himself, but was also a respected editor and anthologist, has said: "After Lear, the limerick grew fantastically. It embraced every topic, territory and temperament; nothing was too sacred or too obscene for those five small lines. The limerick absorbed solemnities and absurdities, traditional legends and off-colour jokes, devout reflections and downright indecencies, without a quiver of the loss of a syllable."

Another writer, HI Brock summed it all up:
Nothing human is excluded from its range. In politics, divinity, philosophy, philology, sociology, zoology; in botany Latinity, relativity, revelry and ribaldry; it is equally at home. Geography is its happy hunting ground. Matters vegetable, animal and mineral are grist to its mill. Love, sacred and profane, is fair game. Bishops and tabby cats are equal targets. And the follies, foibles, fortunes, failures and fallacies to which our mortal flesh is heir, from the cradle to the grave, are the stuff to which its antics give the *coup de pied*.

The popularity of the limerick led naturally to the publication of numerous books. The earliest collection of erotic limericks is believed to have been the twelve-page *New Book of Nonsense* in London in 1868 – surely a gentle sideswipe at Lear! Other titles quickly followed: *Heated Limericks*, *Forbidden Limericks*, *Lusty Limericks & Bawdy Ballads*, and *Pornographia Literaria* which, between them, must have ejaculated a veritable torrent of interesting and erotic scenarios upon the literary society of the day. Ironically, only a couple of years after Lear's death, in 1888, the word "limerick" made its first appearance in the Oxford English Dictionary, defined as "an indecent nonsense verse"!

The Limerick, edited by American Gershon Legman, the first substantial modern collection of bawdy limericks was published in Paris in 1953. More than 500 pages contained almost 1,800 examples, many of them though very poor. Legman himself apologized for this in his introduction to the book: "The prejudices, cruelty, and humourless quality of many of the limericks included are deeply regretted." Precisely why he decided to include them in the first place is anyone's guess. Chapter headings included: *Organs, Strange Intercourse, Oral Irregularities, Abuses of the Clergy, Excrement, Sex Substitutes* and *Assorted Eccentricities*.

Presumably to protect their reputations and accomplishments in other fields, many authors of filthy verses have chosen to hide behind pseudonyms or even complete anonymity. But there have been, and indeed are those others who are perfectly happy – admittedly now in a more modern, broad-minded cultural climate – to be openly associated with their own more risqué outpourings.

Norman Douglas (1868–1952) was an Austrian-born British writer, who lived much of his life abroad – variously in Italy and the south of France, but chiefly on the isle of Capri. While working in the diplomatic service, Douglas was placed on leave in mysterious circumstances, hinting at some sort of sexual scandal. He bought a villa in Naples and married a cousin, with whom he produced two children before divorcing within five years on the grounds of her infidelity.

Among his acquaintances, Douglas counted Graham Greene, food writer Elizabeth David and DH Lawrence. Lawrence apparently upset his friend when he made him the basis of a questionable character is his novel *Aaron's Rod*. In 1928, possibly piqued by Lawrence's success with *Lady Chatterley's Lover*, Douglas published *Some Limericks*, a collection of obscene verses analysed in a mock-serious fashion. A classic of its kind, it has been frequently republished, often in pirate editions.

Isaac Asimov (1920–92) was a Russian-born American author and professor of biochemistry, widely known and highly regarded for his works of science fiction. Asimov was one of the most prolific writers of all time, having written or edited more than 500 books, after selling his first stories, from the age of nineteen, to pulp magazines such as *Amazing Stories* and *Astounding Science Fiction*.

In later life, Asimov also published two collections of bawdy limericks including his most accomplished: *Lecherous Limericks* in 1975, and another book containing precisely 144 verses which reflected his love of puns in its clever title: *Limericks: Too Gross*.

He cultivated an image of himself as an amiable lecher. In the early 1970s, as a response to the popularity of sexual guidebooks such as *The Sensuous Woman* by "J", and *The Sensuous Man* by "M", Asimov published *The Sensuous Dirty Old Man* under the byline "Dr A" although his name was prominently displayed on the cover.

Considering himself to be a feminist well before Women's Liberation became a widespread movement, he nevertheless joked that he wished women to be free because "I hate it when they charge". Interestingly, considering his indisputable intellectual abilities, he truly felt that a good joke could do more to provoke thought than hours of philosophical discussion.

Ironically, despite Asimov's effortless capacity to produce bawdy limericks, he was often criticized for the paucity of strong female characters and lack of sex generally in his science fiction.

John Slim, a Worcester man who lives appropriately in a village called Lickey End, and who has provided many of the verses in this collection, claims to have written more limericks that anyone else in the world – over 8,000 altogether! He must compose in his sleep! His ten published books are testimony to this extraordinary accomplishment. Though it has been suggested that they should, *The Guinness Book of Records* so far have, inexplicably, shown no inclination to acknowledge his amazing achievement within their pages. More fool them!

More modest, and certainly less prolific, authors of bawdy verses include Gerard Benson, Cyril Bibby, Carol Anne Davis, Reg Lynes, Cyril Ray, Frank Richards, Ron Rubin, Stanley J Sharpless, Mike Spilligan, Janet Smith, Nick Toczek, Tom Wayts and countless others all of whom have contributed, and in many cases are still adding, to the enormous continually-growing filthy limerick archive. New funnier, cleverer, even dirtier verses have the satisfying and delightful habit of popping up, as if from nowhere, all the time.

As if proof were needed, here's a brand-new limerick I'd never heard before until recently; whispered unexpectedly in my ear, in the Lounge Bar of The Cripple Creek Tavern, by a very posh lady:

> A friend has an end to his member,
> That, once seen, one would always remember;
>   The size of this knob's
>   Too big for most gobs,
> So, cock-sucking is off the agenda!

In the Foreword to his *Book of Limericks,* published in Paris in 1955, Count Palmiro Vicarion (widely believed to be the pseudonym of poet Christopher Logue) insisted:

> The limerick is precious, an exquisite thing; like a good burgundy, it should not be taken indifferently, too often, or in unduly large quantities. Only a fool, I repeat, a fool would gulp down a glass of Chambertin, or read this book in a sitting...

Glyn Rees

1.
A Sultry Damsel from Delhi, a Disgusting Old Bastard from Nice, and Other Foreign Filth

When we went to a bistro in Cannes,
That is, me and my girlfriend Joanne,
    The garçon, the swine,
    Dipped his dick in the wine,
And offered Joanne coq-au-vin!

There's a pretty young girl, in Ostend,
Whose cunt has a curious bend;
    She's great for a fuck,
    Only then you are stuck
With a prick with a crick in the end!

MICHAEL SWAN

There was a young lady of Nantes,
Who was *tres joli et piquante*,
    But her thing was so small
    It was no good at all,
Except for *la plume de ma tante*.

There was a young man from Peru,
Whose lineage was noble all through;
    It's surely not crud,
    For not only his blood
But even his semen was blue!

There was an old maid from Bermuda,
Who shot a marauding intruder;
    It wasn't her ire
    At his lack of attire,
But he reached for her jewels as he screwed her.

There was a young man from Madras,
Who was stuffing a maid in the grass,
   Though the tropical sun
   Spoilt much of his fun,
By singeing the hairs on his ass.

There was a young man of Hong Kong,
Who sported a metre of dong;
   It looked, when erect,
   Just as one might expect,
Though when rolled up did not seem so long.

There once was a girl of Siam,
Who said to her sweetheart, Kiam:
   "If you take me, of course,
   You must do it by force,
But God knows you're stronger than I am!"

A remarkable race are the Persians:
They embrace such peculiar diversions;
   They make love all day
   In the usual way,
And save, till the nights, their perversions.

A virile young warrior of Palma,
Leapt straight into bed with his charmer;
   She, naturally nude,
   Said: "Please, don't think me rude,
But I do wish you'd take off your armour!"

Vodka's the stuff for the Reds,
It seems not to go to their heads:
   While the girls wash their smalls in it,
   The boys dunk their balls in it,
Before leaping into their beds.

CYRIL RAY

Chimed a charming young hussy of Padua:
"A peso! Why, sir, what a cadua!"
   He said, raising his hat:
   "You're not worth even that.
I am, however, glad to have hadua!"

The girls of Bordeaux, I'm afraid,
You would hardly consider as staid:
   A young Bordelaise
   Knows of dozens of ways
In which she can get bordelaide...

CYRIL RAY

"Monsieur Gauguin? E's gone to Tahiti,
Where ze girls are so friendly and preety;
   'E paints them *tout* bare
   Wiz zair lovely black 'air
And bodies so 'ow you say? meaty!"

SJ SHARPLESS

There was a young man of Eau Claire,
Enjoying his girl on the stair;
   On the forty-fourth stroke
   The banister broke,
And he finished her off in mid-air!

In the shade of a palm tree at Sousse,
He said: "*J'aime tes deux pamplemousses.*"*
   With languorous sigh
   She murmured reply:
"*Je pense que ta banane est douce*".†

* *"I love your two grapefruits."*
† *"I think your banana is sweet."*

21

On an outing with seventeen Czechs,
A young tour guide supplied the free sex;
    She returned from the jaunt
    Feeling, well – slightly gaunt,
But the Czechs were all absolute wrecks!

        The Kings of Peru were the Incas,
        Who were known far and wide as great drincas;
            They worshipped the sun,
            And had loads of great fun,
        Though their rivals considered them stincas!

A nudist resort, in Benares,
Took a midget in all unawares;
    But he made members weep,
    For he just couldn't keep
His nose out of others' affairs.

There was a young lady of Burma
Who sighed: "I must try to be firmer;
    But whenever I try
    To say 'No!' to a guy,
It seems to be 'Yes' that I murmur…"

RON RUBIN

        There was a young man of Calcutta
        Who tried to write "cunt" on a shutter;
            He'd managed c-u-
            When a pious Hindu
        Knocked him arse-over-tit in the gutter.

When a girl, on an island remote,
Met a Frenchman who lived in a boat,
   She was soon in his bunk
   With a mouthful of spunk,
And a bloody great frog in her throat!

        A senorita who strolled on the Corso,
        Displayed quite a lot of her torso;
           A crowd soon collected,
           And no one objected,
        Though some were in favour of more so.

A girl, who was touring Zambezi,
Said: "Attracting the chaps is so easy:
   I don't wear any pants,
   And, when given the chance,
Simply stand where it's frightfully breezy!"

There was a young man of Belgrade,
Who planned to seduce a fair maid;
   And as it befell,
   He succeeded quite well,
And the maid, like the plan, was well-laid.

ISAAC ASIMOV

        The French are a race among races:
        They will screw in the funniest places;
           Any orifice handy
           Is considered quite dandy –
        That's including the one in their faces!

An idle young wanker from Rheims,
Can't be bothered to delve in his jeans;
  This lamentable loafer
  Just sleeps on the sofa,
And prefers to rely on wet dreams.

     A publisher visited France,
     In search of a tale of romance;
       A Parisian lady
       Told a story so shady,
     He made an immediate advance.

As two consular clerks in Madras,
Fished, hidden in deepest shore-grass:
  "What a marvellous pole,"
  She remarked, "But control
Your sinkers – they're banging my ass!"

     There's an unbroken babe from Toronto,
     Who's exceedingly hard to come onto;
       But when you get there,
       And have parted her hair,
     You may fuck her as much as you want to.

A rumbustious rake from Stamboul,
Felt his ardour grow suddenly cool;
  No lack of affection
  Reduced his erection –
His zipper got snagged on his tool!

There was a sweet girl from Alaska
Who'd fuck anyone who would ask her;
   She perfected her vice,
   And, thus, shot up in price,
So that no one could touch her but Jesus H Christ,
Or possibly John Jacob Astor.

To succeed in the brothels at Derna,
One must always begin as a learner;
   Indentured at six,
   As a greaser of pricks,
One may rise to be fitter and turner.

Said a girl from Staraya Russa,
Whom the war had made looser and looser:
   "Yes, I'm wormin' a German,
   A vermin called Herman,
But his dink is a lollapalooza!"

There was a young man from Siam,
Who said: "I go in with a wham!
   But I soon lose my starch,
   Like the mad month of March,
And the lion comes out like a lamb."

A vicious old whore from Albania,
Hated men with a terrible mania;
   With a twitch and a squirm,
   She would hold back your sperm,
And then roll on her face and disdain yer.

Said a frustrated gal in Valletta:
"Our love life perhaps might be better;
  If we don't have it off
  Until after I doff
My bra, pants, jeans, thermals and sweater!"

There was a young man of Jaipur,
Whose cock was shot off in the war;
  So he's painted the front
  To resemble a cunt,
And has set himself up as a whore.

Quite unique is a strumpet of Mazur,
In the way that her clientele pays her:
  A machine that she uses,
  Fastens on to her whoosis,
And records everybody that lays her!

An Italian waitress named Cora,
Has discovered that diners adore a
  Plump titty that's ripe,
  And a cunt that's like tripe –
Now she doesn't wait tables no more-a!

A newlywed couple from Goshen,
Spent their honeymoon sailing the ocean;
   In thirty-one days,
   They got laid eighty ways –
Just imagine such fucking devotion!

An earnest young woman in Thrace,
Cried out: "Darling, that's not the right place!"
   So he gave her a smack,
   And performed round the back
What he couldn't have done face to face.

There was a young man of Cape Horn,
Who wished he had never been born,
    And he wouldn't have been,
    If his father had seen
That the end of the rubber was torn.

        A knight, while crusading in Palma,
        Laid a lady who'd thought him a charmer;
            The damsel, though crushed,
            Chastely blushed at what gushed
        From his dink through a chink in his armour.
        JOHN SLIM

There was a young lad from Nahant,
Who was made like the Sensitive Plant;
    When asked: "Do you fuck?"
    He replied: "No such luck –
I would if I could but I can't."

        There was a young fellow of Perth,
        Whose balls were the finest on earth;
            They grew to such size,
            That they each won a prize,
        And God only knows what they were worth!

There was a young man of Natal,
And Sue was the name of his gal;
    One day, north of Aden,
    He got his hard rod in,
And came clear up Suez canal.

There is a young man in Darjeeling,
Whose member extends to the ceiling;
    It pops out of his pocket
    Into the light socket –
My God! What a wonderful feeling!

There was a young man from Eurasia,
Who toasted his balls in a brazier;
    Till they grew quite as hot,
    As the glamorous twat,
Of Miss Diana Digby-Duff Frazier.

A Parisian actor called Alec,
Wrote a postcard, romantic and Gallic,
    But then went one better
    And sent a French letter –
Quite equally Gallic, but phallic!

A cheerful old party of Lucknow,
Remarked: "I should much like a fuck now!"
    So he had one and spent,
    And said: "There, I'm content,
But by no means am I so cunt-struck now!"

A young senorita from Spain,
Though her face was uncommonly plain,
    Had a cunt with a pucker
    That made the men fuck her
Again, and again, and again. (And again!)

A bored little girl from Peru,
Who had nothing whatever to do,
    Sat quite still on the stairs,
    Counting short, curly hairs –
Several thousand, four hundred and two!

      There was a young girl of Asturias,
      With a penchant for practices curious;
         She loved to bat rocks,
           With her gentlemen's cocks –
      An activity rude and injurious!

An adventurous chap from Norway,
Tried to jack himself off in a sleigh;
    But the air was that frigid,
    It froze his balls rigid,
And all he could come was frappé.

      A forthright young bride, a Canuck,
      Told her man: "We must do more than suck.
         I think it's time, maybe,
         To have our first baby –
      So, abandon this Frenching, let's fuck!"

There once was a Spanish nobilio,
Who lived in a Spanish castilio;
    More often than not,
    His cojones got hot,
At the thought of a Spanish jazzilio.

An innocent lad in Lapland,
Was informed fornication was grand;
    But at his first trial,
    He remarked, with a smile:
"I've had similar feelings – by hand!"

An evil young man from Khartoum,
Had enticed a poor girl to his room;
    He not only fucked her,
    But buggered and sucked her –
And left her to pay for the room!

A skinny old maid from Verdun,
Wed a short-peckered son-of-a-gun;
    Said she: "I don't care
    If there ain't that much there –
Goodness knows some is better than none!"

There was a young girl from Sofia,
Who succumbed to her lover's desire;
   Said she: "It's a sin,
   But, well – now that it's in,
Could you shove it a few inches higher?"

Alas for the Countess d'Isere,
Whose poor muff was not furnished with hair;
   Said the Count: "*Quelle surprise!*"
   When he parted her thighs;
"*Magnifique! Pourtant pas de la guerre.*"*

* "*Magnificent! However, not from the war*"

A reckless young lady of France
Had no qualms about taking a chance;
 But she felt it was crude,
 To get screwed in the nude,
So she always went home with damp pants.

There was a young girl from Hong Kong,
Who remarked: "You're entirely wrong,
 To declare my vagina,
 The largest in China,
On account of your minuscule dong."

Asked a man of a maid of Ashanti:
"Can one sniff of your twitchet, or can't he?"
 Said she, with a grin:
 "Of course! Shove it in!
But *presto* please – not too *andante*."

There was a young girl in Berlin,
Who was fucked by an elderly Finn;
 Though he diddled his best,
 And performed with such zest,
She kept wondering: "Pop, is it in?"

There was a young lady of Paris,
Whom nothing could ever embarrass,
   Till, that is, one day,
   In a sidewalk café,
She abruptly ran into Frank Harris.*

*FRANK HARRIS (1856–1931) *was an author remembered mainly for his memoir* My Life and Loves, *which was banned in many countries on account of its sexually explicit nature.*

Said a horrible whore of Lahore,
Whilst ape-fucking against a barn door:
   "This orang-utang
   Is much better than bhang –
I just can't get enough, give me more!"

A Welshman who ate some Caerphilly,
Said: "I love Wales because it's so hilly;
   The girls in the valley
   Are ever so pally –
They shout: 'Show us your... don't be so silly!'"

There was a fat lady of China,
Who'd a really enormous vagina;
   And when she was dead,
   They painted it red,
And used it for docking a liner.

An accomplished young lady from Brussels,
Was so proud of her vaginal muscles;
   She could easily plex them
   And so interflex them
As to whistle love songs through her bustles.

      There was a young girl of Carolina,
      With a very capricious vagina;
         To the shock of one fucker
         It pursed into a pucker,
      And whistled the chorus from "Dinah".

A hirsute old queen of Bulgaria,
Had a bush that had grown ever hairier;
   Till a prince from Peru,
   Who'd arrived for a screw,
Had to hunt for her cunt with his terrier.

35

A fraulein from Altstadt-am-Rhein,
Was groped in a call-box in Tyne;
  When the pest wouldn't leave her,
  She grabbed the receiver,
And yelled down the phone: "*Nein! Nein! Nein!*"

RON RUBIN

A bounder in far St Domingo,
Being tired of sex, said: "By jingo!
  Blast all women and boys,
  I shall try some new toys."
And he went out and fucked a flamingo!

There was a young lady of Rhodes,
Who sinned in unusual modes;
  At the height of her fame.
  She abruptly became
The proud mother of three dozen toads!

An insatiable girl from Odessa,
Is a somewhat unblushing transgressor,
  When referred to the priest,
  The lewd little beast
Began to undress her confessor!

A well-behaved girl from Samoa,
Was determined that no man would know her;
   One young fellow tried,
   But she wriggled aside,
And spilled all the spermatozoa.

A frustrated young bride in St Remo,
Stayed as chaste as the holy bambino;
   For she'd married a slicker
   So fond of his liquor,
He ignored her sweet, ripe maraschino.

     A young lad from Auckland called PeeWee,
     Once managed to train his pet kiwi
        To tap-tap-tap-tap
        When it needed a crap,
     And wink when it wanted a wee-wee.

RON RUBIN

An old dowager near Sweden's Landing,
Is regarded as very demanding;
   It is one of her jests
   To suck off her guests –
She just hates to keep gentlemen standing.

An unfortunate maiden from Klepper,
Spent an ill-fated night with a stepper;
   And now, in dismay,
   She mutters each day:
"His pee-pee was made of red-pepper!"

An immature chap from Racine,
Is still breast-feeding, nearly sixteen;
   He says: "I admit
   There's no milk in the tit,
But think of the fun it has been!"

In La France a persuasive young man,
Wooed a girl on the beach down at Cannes;
   Said the mademoiselle:
   "*Eh, monsieur, vot ze 'ell?*
Stay away from where *zere's no sontan*!"

There was an old chap from Tagore,
Whose tool was a yard long, or more;
   So he wore the damn thing
   In a surgical sling,
To prevent it from sweeping the floor!

An elderly chappie named Harris,
Who spent a long weekend in Paris,
   Eventually fell
   For no mademoiselle,
But a tart from Carmarthen called Carys!

There's a generous girl in Tobruk,
Who considers her quiff as a nook;
   It's so deep and so wide,
   You can curl up inside
On a nice easy chair with a book.

There was a young stud from Stamboul,
Who boasted so torrid a tool,
   That each female crater
   Explored by this satyr,
Seemed almost unpleasantly cool.

A frustrated chap from Calcutta,
Lost his patience and ventured to mutter:
   "If her Bartholin glands
   Don't respond to my hands,
I shall have to resort to fresh butter!"

A young girl named Alice, in Dallas,
Had never enjoyed a fine phallus;
   She was virgo intacto,
   Because, ipso facto,
No phallus in Dallas fit Alice.

A lady from far Madagascar
Consented to marry a Lascar;
   Her friends thought her naughty,
   But she was past forty,
And he was the first man to ask her.

      My girlfriend who lives down in Dallas is
      Studying psychoanalysis;
         Whenever I straddle her,
         She prates about Adler,
      But at least she's found out what a phallus is!
      RON RUBIN

A most fortunate guy from Toledo,
Has been blessed with excessive libido;
   To fuck and to screw,
   And to fornicate, too,
Are the three major points of his credo.

      A lassie who lived in Virginny,
      Had a cunt that could bark, neigh and whinny;
         The county set claimed her,
         But success overcame her,
      As her tone became harsher, and tinny.

A generous tart from Johore,
Loved to lie on a mat on the floor;
   In a manner uncanny,
   She'd wriggle her fanny,
And drain your nuts dry to the core.

An old cop from Death Valley Junction,
Whose organ had long ceased to function,
   Deceived his poor wife,
   For the rest of her life,
With the dexterous use of his truncheon.

A pansy who lived in Khartoum,
Took a lesbian up to his room,
   But they argued a lot
   About who would do what,
And quite how and with what and to whom.

A hot-tempered girl from Caracas,
Was wed to a samba-mad jackass;
   When he started to cheat her
   With a dark senorita,
She drop-kicked him in the maracas.

A handful of reasons the Poles,
Always do well in sexual polls:
   Their balls (quite immense),
   And the size and the strength
And the length of their prehensile poles!

There was a young lady from Wales,
Who had visited France to eat snails;
   She swallowed a score,
   Though it felt a lot more –
She'd been given a bowl full of males.

ANNE WILKS

A lad, christened William Winkie,
Walked the wintry streets of Helsinki,
   With not a stitch on,
   And the wind blowing strong –
Hence his nickname of Wee Willie Winkie!

One midnight, old DG Rossetti,
Remarked to Miss Sidall: "Oh, Betty,
   I wish that you'd stop
   Shouting, 'Fuck me, you wop!' –
It turna da tool to spaghetti!"

VICTOR GRAY

There was an old man from Rwanda,
Who attempted to bugger a gander;
　　But that virtuous bird
　　Plugged its ass with a turd,
And refused to such low tastes to pander.

An Athenian singer called Nina,
Was partial, it seems, to Retsina;
　　She's been all the rage
　　Since she staggered on stage,
And stripped to a slow cavatina.

RON RUBIN

Said the thoughtful Chief Rabbi of Joppa:
"I believe circumcision's improper
　　If the organ is small;
　　But I don't mind at all
About taking a slice off a whopper!"

There was a young chap from Lahore,
Whose prick was an inch, and no more;
　　It was all right for keyholes,
　　And smaller girls' pee-holes,
But not worth a damn with a whore.

In Turkey, a chap in a truss,
Caused a fuss on the bus. It was thus:
   He whipped out his whang,
   And offered a bang
To a lady a few seats from us!

JOHN SLIM

A helpful young miss in Tasmania,
Will do all she can to sustainia,
   But once you have shot
   The lot that you've got,
She won't do a thing to detainia.

JOHN SLIM

There was a young maid of Madras,
Who had a magnificent ass:
   Not quite as you think,
   Softly dimpled and pink –
But grey, with four legs and eats grass!

A lovely young thing, of St Kitts,
Lured a lad with her fine pair of tits;
   Now she's thinking of England,
   While the old out-and-in gland
Is chafing her fanny to bits.

A lecher, around Ringaskiddy,
With a dinger not daunting but diddy,
   Drew muted applause
   From scores of bored whores,
But cheered up a grateful old biddy!

Yet one more picturesque coastal village!
I'm exhausted with raping and pillage;
   I enjoy sex, of course.
   After all, I am Norse,
But don't expect any seminal spillage!

There is a young lady of Quimper,
Whose strength is concealed in her simper,
    Many a gang
    Comes by for a bang,
But soon staggers out with a whimper!

JOHN SLIM

There once was a maiden of Ottowa,
Whose husband, she said, thought a lot of her;
    Which, to give him his due,
    Was most probably true,
Since he'd sired twenty kids, all begot of her!

A stripper who came from Ozinki,
Displayed curves both sultry and slinky;
    And then got the chaps
    In a state of collapse
As she moved from the cute to the kinky.

JOHN SLIM

A naughty young nympho, in Norway,
Hung nude (upside down) in a doorway;
    She told her young man:
    "Have what fun you can,
And next time we'll do something your way!"

I'm a little batty

A kindly young lady of Lille,
Would charge you a *franc* for a feel,
    Or she'd help you to wank,
    But that would be *cinq*,
And anything more was a *mille*.

An honest young man in Helsinki,
Gave a tart a lascivious wink, he
    Said: "Let's have a go,
    Though I think you should know
That my dink, for a dink, is quite dinky."

JOHN SLIM

    She is known to be prone to invite,
    Gentlemen who will visit, at night,
        In far Guatemala –
        You go through the parlour,
    Up the stairs, second door on the right.

A wistful young lady, in Garda,
When in bed said: "I'm sure it was harder,
    Till I made it produce
    An abundance of juice
When you came, in our game, in the Lada!"

    There was an old German, called Rosen,
    Who liked to wear short lederhosen;
        "Although they look cute on,"
        He said, "A young Teuton,
    In winter my schwanz gets quite frozen!"

    RON RUBIN

A beautiful bint, from Brazil,
Could alter her slot size at will;
    It would stretch, or else shrink
    To embrace any dink,
And ensure she was getting her fill!

JOHN SLIM

When Tom lost his Dad in Biarritz,
He tickled the gendarmes to bits:
    "*Ma foi*! What's he like?"
    They asked the young tyke –
"Jack Daniels and birds with big tits!"

A buxom young dancer called Cleo
Did cabaret way down in Rio;
   Each night when she rhumba'd,
   Her breasts, unencumbered
By corsage, would join in *con brio*.

RON RUBIN

An eager young man, from Belize,
Makes love with his ladies in threes;
   He's no inhibitions
   Regarding positions,
And asks them to come as they please.

A bride in Bangkok got a shock:
Raised veins in big rings round his cock;
    She found, when well bedded,
    She'd got him cross-threaded –
The fire brigade's still taking stock.

A lusty young lad of renown,
Made tourists in Austria frown:
    He'd slip it inside
    On a cable-car ride,
And, again, get it up coming down!

JOHN SLIM

There was a young man of Ancona,
Who'd not bonked his bird since he'd known her;
    She asked him to try,
    But he said: "DIY
Is my usual thing – I'm a loner!"

Said a pious young bride of Toledo,
To her groom: "You must honour my credo:
    To ensure an immaculate
    Conception, please ejaculate
Without taking Off Your Tuxedo!"

RON RUBIN

A kindly old harlot from China,
Could not have a policy finer:
   So poor men won't holler,
   She charges one dollar,
And twenty-five cents for a minor.

      A young window-cleaner, Luigi,
      Was screwing a lady from Fiji;
         When she broke into a sweat,
         He said: "Don't worry, pet!"
      And squeezed off the excess with his squeegee.

An old Admiral, stationed in Nanking,
Was quite clearly partial to spanking;
   He remarked: "S & M
   Is so good for us men –
It's a far better option than wanking!"

      At Vassar sex isn't injurious,
      Though of love we are never penurious.
         Though we may die old maids,
         Thanks to vulcanized aids
      At least we shall never die curious.

A haughty young wench of Del Norte,
Would fuck only men over forty;
   Said she: "It's too quick
   With a novice's prick,
I prefer it to last, and be warty!"

"My brain," claims a student from Rome,
"Is my biggest erogenous zone."
    Quite a novel idea,
    Though the reason, I fear,
Why she spends so much time on her own!

A mademoiselle, from Marseilles,
Asked what she did during the day,
    Replied: "Entertain –
    Although never for gain,
And nothing remotely risqué!"

ELEANOR ROGERS

I met a lewd nude in Bermuda,
Who thought she was shrewd, I was shrewder;
    She considered it crude
    To be wooed in the nude –
I pursued her, subdued her, and screwed her.

There was a young girl of Baroda,
Who built an erotic pagoda;
    The walls of its halls
    Were festooned with the balls
And the tools of the fools who bestrode her.

There was old roué from Rome,
Who took a young leprechaun home;
    As he buggered the elf,
    He thought to himself:
"I'd be much better off with a gnome!"

Hell's Angels, en route through Pretoria,
Gang-banged a young virgin named Gloria;
　　That was two weeks ago,
　　And, as far as we know,
She is still in a state of euphoria.

A disgusting old bastard from Nice,
Who'd successfully fucked several geese,
　　Went a smidgen too far
　　With the budgerigar,
And his parrot alerted the police!

I'd like to
report a birdlary

A young Spaniard who's hung like a horse,
Is first-choice with the ladies, of course;
    They long for a dong
    That can bong a huge gong –
So this Juan is their primary source.

    A yogi in far-off Beirut,
    For women does not care a hoot;
        But his organ will stand
        In a manner quite grand
    When a snake-charmer tootles his flute.

There was a young sailor from Rome,
Who found the girls over the foam,
    All acted the same
    In the sexual game,
So he might just as well have stayed home.

    A sultry young damsel from Delhi,
    Who exotically wriggled her belly,
        Inspired, through her dance,
        Chaps to fancy their chance –
    Though she told them all: "Not on your nelly!"

ELEANOR ROGERS

There was a young lady from France,
Who jumped on a bus in a trance;
  Six passengers fucked her,
  Besides the conductor,
Whilst the driver came (twice) in his pants.

There was a young maiden of Joppa,
Who became a society cropper;
  She went off to Ostend
  With a gentleman friend,
And the rest of the story's improper.

A lovely French girl, from Calais,
Looks great in her sheer negligée;
  Delightful and chaste,
  She would just suit the taste
Of a typical Gallic gourmet.

There was an old man from the Nile,
Whose sexual habits were vile;
  Yet whenever he'd score,
  The woman all swore
That he sure made perversion worthwhile.

ISAAC ASIMOV

A young teacher from far-off Bombay,
Turned down a request for a lay,
   (Nicely couched in a note),
   Since the fellow who wrote,
Had spelled "intercoarse" with an "a".

ISAAC ASIMOV

        A fastidious fop of Bhogat,
        Often sucked a girl's pussy, like that,
           Though he'd wipe off her jib,
           As he'd put on a bib
        To ensure he'd not soil his cravat.

There was a young lady from Perth,
Who cried "I'm increasing in girth!"
   And her fine, divine figure
   Grew steadily bigger
And bigger and bigger, 'til birth.

2.
Exhibitionist Annie, her Fanny, and Other Strumpets, Virgins and Brides

There is a young lady named Aird,
Whose bottom is always kept bared;
   When asked why, she pouts,
   And says the Boy Scouts
All beg her to please Be Prepared.

      There was a young girl, a sweet lamb,
      Who smiled as she entered the tram;
         And when she'd embarked,
         The conductor remarked:
      "Your fare", and she said: "Yes, I am!"

When a young lass got married, in Bicester,
Her mother remarked, as he kissed her:
   "This fellow you've won
   Is bound to be fun –
He's already fucked me and your sister!"

      A provocative temptress, named Claire,
      Remarked, as she sprawled in a chair:
         "I can tell by your glance
         I've forgotten my pants –
      OK, stare at me bare, I don't care!"

In a launderette, waiting to rinse,
A poor innocent fellow named Vince
   Saw delightful Miss Dyer
   Put her drawers in the drier,
And he hasn't been quite the same since!

A Colonial girl, sweet and sainted,
Was by war-striped young Indians tainted;
   When asked of the ravages,
   She said of the savages:
"They ain't half as bad as they're painted!"

       Softly seductive young Brenda,
       Wants a man who is sweet, kind and tender,
          And thoughtful and bright,
          And sexually right –
       But mostly a very big spender!

An attractive young girl from Key West,
Was exceptionally large in the chest;
   Her boyfriend's attention
   To her outsize dimension
Brought his own measurement to its best.

       Kind sir, please address me as Mabel,
       And though I'm not certain I'm able,
          I am willing to try,
          Therefore, where shall I lie –
       On the bed, on the floor, or the table?

She entertains men of all nations,
Causing various lustful sensations;
   When asked: "Are those dozens
   Of callers your cousins?"
She responds: "No, just sexual relations!"

Said a calendar pin-up, named Gloria:
"So the boys may enjoy true euphoria,
   You must pose as you are
   During Jan, Feb and Mar,
And, in April, they'll wanna see moria!"

      A cautious young girl, from Penzance,
      Decided to take one small chance:
         She wavered, then lo,
         She let herself go...
      Now all of her sisters are aunts!

There is a young maid, from Kilkenny,
Who is bothered by lovers so many
   That the saucy young elf
   Plans to raffle herself,
And the tickets are four for a penny!

There was a young girl from Decatur,
Who sailed out to sea on a freighter;
   She was screwed by the master,
   An utter disaster,
Which the crew all made up for much later.

      A willing young girl, named Cervantes,
      Cried: "Of course you may poke in my panties!
         And I'd draw the line
         If the panties were mine,
      But they aren't my panties, they're Aunty's!"

The typists at Wheesley & Beesley,
All fornicate freely and easily;
   In this pleasant way
   They can add to their pay,
Which, at Wheesley & Beesley, is measley!

Once bedded, your militant miss
Is quite likely to say, with a hiss:
   "I assure you we sisters
   Would kick out you misters,
If we didn't need that to do this!"

MICHAEL FLINT

A handsome young launderess, named Spangle,
Had tits tilting up at an angle;
   "They may tickle my chin,"
   She confessed, with a grin,
"But at least they stay clear of the mangle!"

Some gels, and I don't understand 'em,
Will strip off their clothing at random,
   Without any qualms,
   To exhibit their charms –
In short *quod erat demonstrandum*.

A Boy Scout was having his fill,
Of a nice little Brownie, near Rhyl;
   "We must Be Prepared,"
   Said Patrol Leader Aird,
"So my girls are all taking the pill!"

There was a young trollop from Trent,
Who claimed not to know what they meant –
   When a man asked her age,
   She'd reply, in a rage:
"Why, my age is the age of consent!"

There was a young lady of Norwood,
Whose ways were provokingly forward;
   Said her mother: "My dear,
   You wiggle, I fear,
Your posterior just like a whore would!"

There was a young squaw of Chokdunt,
Who had an adjustable cunt;
   Though it had many uses,
   It made no papooses,
And fitted both giant and runt.

There was a young girl from Eskdale,
Who offered her sweet ass for sale;
   For the sum of two bits
   You could tickle her tits,
But a dollar would get you some tail.

     A wanton young lady, of Wimley,
     Reproached for not acting more primly,
        Answered: "Heavens Above!
        I know sex isn't love,
     But it's such an attractive facsimile!"

There's an over-sexed lady called White,
Who insists on a dozen per night;
   A fellow named Cheddar
   Had the brashness to wed her –
His chance of survival is slight.

     Every time Lady Lowbodice swoons,
     Her plump boobies pop out like balloons;
        But her butler stands by,
        With hauteur in his eye,
     And lifts them back in with warm spoons.

A naked young tart named Roselle,
Walked the pavements while ringing a bell;
   When asked why she rang it,
   She answered: "God, dang it!
Can't you see I've got something to sell?"

There was an old maid of Pitlochry,
Whose morals were truly a mockery;
   For, under the bed,
   Was a lover, instead
Of the usual porcelain crockery!

There was a young maiden, from Multerry,
Whose knowledge of life was desultory;
  She explained, like a sage:
  "Adolescence? The stage
Between puberty and, er – adultery!"

      There was a young lady of Maine,
      Who declared she'd a man on the brain;
        But you knew from the view
        Of her waist as it grew,
      It was not on her brain he had lain.

There once was a lady called Mabel,
Always ready, and willing, and able;
  And so full of spice,
  She could name her own price –
There goes Mabel, all wrapped up in sable!

      An amorous lady named Lilly,
      Walked the pavements of old Piccadilly;
        She remarked: "Ain't it funny,
        It's not for the money –
      But if I don't take it, it's silly!"

There was an old tart, from Kilkenny,
Whose usual charge was a penny;
  For half of that sum,
  You might fondle her bum –
A source of amusement to many!

There was a young lady named Kate,
Who necked in the dark with her date;
   When asked how she'd fared,
   She said she was scared,
But otherwise doing first-rate!

      It always delights me, in Lancs,
      To stroll on the old canal banks;
         One time, in long grass,
         I stepped on an ass,
      And heard a young girl murmur: "Thanks!"

There once was a maid with such graces,
That her curves cried aloud for embraces;
   "You look," cried each he,
   "Like a million to me –
And invested in all the right places!"

      On oysters washed down with Frascati,
      You can make a girl act rather tarty –
         A very good wheeze
         If you'd like her to please
      As the life and the soul of the party...
      CYRIL RAY

A wartime young lady of fashion,
Much noted for wit and for passion,
   Is known to have said,
   As she jumped into bed:
"Here's one thing those bastards won't ration!"

A girl doesn't need to be witty,
Or even especially pretty,
    So long as she'll share
    My glass whilst I bare
The snowy delights of her bosom...

CYRIL RAY

A desperate spinster, from Clare,
Once knelt on the front lawn, quite bare;
    She prayed to her God
    For a romp on the sod –
And a gardener answered her prayer.

There was a young lady named Eva,
Who filled up her bath to receive her;
    She took off her clothes,
    From her head to her toes,
And a voice through the keyhole yelled: "Beaver!"

A curvaceous young lady named Etta,
Always chose to be clad in a sweater;
    Three reasons she had –
    Keeping warm was not bad,
But the other two reasons were better!

        The family party grew merrier,
        Its passions excited by Perrier,
           And on bumpers of Vichy,
           Even Grandma looked dishy
        And showed signs of erotic hysteria...

        CYRIL RAY

        An ample young lady of Eton,
        Whose figure had plenty of meat on,
           Said: "Marry me, dear,
           And you'll find that my rear
        Is a nice place to warm your cold feet on!"

"I cannot be bothered with drawers!"
Insists one of our better-known whores;
    "There isn't much doubt,
    I do better without
In conducting my day-to-day chores!"

A lisping young lady named Beth,
Was saved from a fate worse than death
   Seven times in a row,
   Which unsettled her so,
That she quit saying "No" and said "Yeth!"

A lassie from wee Ballachulish
Observed that: "Virginity's foolish;
   When a lad makes a try,
   To say ought but 'Och, aye!'
Would be stubborn, pig-headed and mulish!"

A lock-keeper's lass, in Upavon,
Had locks that were black as a raven;
   On her head they were straight,
   But they curled near the gate
Which led to the innermost haven.

CYRIL BIBBY

A lady I know, rather merry,
Spilt a whole glass of bubbly perry;
   It made quite a mess
   Down the front of her dress,
But what fun we had finding her cherry!

There was a young girl named Bianca,
Who slept while the ship lay at anchor;
   She awoke in dismay
   When she heard the mate say:
"Now – hoist up the topsheet, and spank her!"

The ladies inhabiting Venus,
Have signalled us, saying they've seen us;
   They add: "There's a yen here
   For getting some men here –
And nothing but space in between us!"

        She sent me a text on my phone:
        "I need fucking, right now – please come home!"
           Other blokes took the call
           (She had copied to all),
        And the queue was the longest I've known.

A prostitute living in London,
Went pantless, with zippers all undone;
   She'd explain: "Well, you see
   I can do two or three,
While Ruby next door's getting one done!"

DOUGLAS CATLEY

A lass of curvaceous physique,
Liked dresses that made her look chic,
   But all could agree
   That topless to knee,
Did little to help her mystique.

DOUGLAS CATLEY

        An innocent bride from the Mission,
        Remarked, on her first night's coition:
          "What an intimate section
          To use for connection,
        And, Lord, what a silly position!"

An agreeable girl, named Miss Doves,
Likes to jack-off the young chaps she loves;
    She will use her bare fist
    If the blighters insist,
But she really prefers to wear gloves.

There was a young bride named McWing,
Who thought sex a delirious fling;
    When her bridegroom grew ill
    From too much (as they will),
She found other men liked the same thing!

Try our Rubber Girlfriend (air-inflatable),
Perennially young (quite insatiable);
   Our satisfied clients,
   From mere midgets to giants,
Say she's incredibly sexy and mate-able.

      A naive young lady of Cork,
      Had been told she was brought by the stork;
         But after a day
         With a gent called O'Shea,
      She was doubtful of that sort of talk.

      REG YEARLEY

Said a luscious young lady, called Wade,
On a beach with her charms all displayed:
   "It's so hot in the sun,
   Perhaps sex would be fun –
Well, at least it would give me some shade!"

      Though his plan, when he gave her a buzz,
      Was to do what a chap chiefly duzz,
         She declared: "I'm a soul,
         Not a sexual goal!"
      So he shrugged, and called someone who wuzz.

To her gardener, a lady named Lilliom,
Said; "Billy, plant roses and trilliom!"
   Then started to fool
   With the gardener's tool,
And wound up in the bed of Sweet William.

There's a very prim girl called McDrood:
What a combo – both nympho and prude!
   She wears her dark glasses
   When fellows make passes,
And keeps her eyes shut when she's screwed.

     Said Miss Farrow, on one of her larks:
     "Sex is more fun in bed than in parks.
       You feel more at ease,
       Your ass doesn't freeze,
     And passers-by don't make remarks."

I wouldn't do it like that

Said a diffident lady named Drood,
The first time she'd observed a chap nude:
   "I'm glad I'm the sex
   That's concave, not convex
For I don't hold with things that protrude!"

When he ravished a maid on a train,
They arrested the fellow to biame;
   But the ex-virgin cried:
   "That's for me to decide,
And I'll be the last to complain!"

Cried a slender young lady called Toni,
With a bottom exceedingly bony:
   "I'll say this for my rump,
   Though it may not be plump,
It's my own, not a silicone phoney!"

There was a young lady, named Frances,
Who decided to better her chances,
   By cleverly adding
   Appropriate padding,
Enlarging her protuberances!

There was an old lady of Leicester,
Who imagined a bounder caressed her;
   All day she would wriggle,
   And jiggle and giggle,
As though seven devils possessed her.

"Last night," said a lassie named Ruth,
"In a long-distance telephone booth,
   I enjoyed the perfection
   Of an ideal connection –
I was screwed, if you must know the truth!"

The delightful young daughter of Herr Finn,
Had voluptuous virginal fair skin.
    When I said to her: "Mabel,
    You'd look so good in sable."
She replied: "I look best in my bare skin!"

There was an old maid of Vancouver,
Who captured a chap by manoeuvre:
    She jumped on his knee
    With some rare *eau de vie*,
And nothing on earth could remove her.

A young lady whose breasts were quite wee,
Little more than the stings of a bee,
    Decided implants
    Were the way to enhance
What's become a vast 52 (Gee!).

A young lass with a prize-winning bum
Entertained all the lads, one by one,
    Till a bugger from Dover
    Said: "Why not turn over,
And we can have twice as much fun!"

A price-conscious hooker, called Annie,
Whose tariff was cheap but quite canny,
    Charged a buck for a fuck,
    Fifty cents for a suck,
And a dime for a feel of her fanny.

A couturier, from Haverfordwest,
Has designed an ankle-length vest;
    She says: "It's got holes
    For respectable souls
Who can only have sex when they're dressed!"

EO PARROTT

Concerning the question of cunts:
You really must see Helen Hunt's;
    With carrots and candles,
    And hockey-stick handles,
She performs some remarkable stunts!

"Give me cock! Give me cock! Give me cock!"
Chants a chick with a mantra to shock;
   There is nothing this hippie
   Likes more than a quickie,
And the queue stretches right round the block.

GARY LUCAS

There is a young girl from Uttoxeter,
An exquisite and passionate cock-sitter;
   With her prehensile hole,
   She envelopes my pole,
And squirms up and down as my rocks hit 'er.

        The usherette down at the Ritz,
        Has a marvellous pair of big tits,
           Which she keeps nice and firm
           By massaging with sperm,
        Whenever her boyfriend permits.

Fuck me quick, fuck me deep, fuck me oft,
In the bog, in the bath, in the loft,
   Up my arse, up my cunt,
   From behind, from in front,
With your best, stiffest cock – nothing soft!

        A hooker of note, called Miss Flux,
        Could command at least two hundred bucks;
           But for that she would suck you,
           And wank you and fuck you –
        The whole thing quite simply De Luxe!

Of my husband I do not ask much,
Just an "all mod and con" little hutch;
    Bank account in my name,
    With the cheque book the same,
Plus a small fee for fucking and such.

        A businesslike harlot named Draper,
        Once tried an unusual caper;
            What made it so nice
            Was you got it half-price
        If you'd cut out her ad from the paper!

Jane said to Linda: "'Do you
And your husband speak during a screw?"
    Linda said, with a groan,
    "If he calls on the phone,
When I'm at it, what else can I do?"

JOHN SLIM

        An apparently shy girl from Pecking
        Would indulge in a great deal of necking,
            Which seemed such a waste,
            Since she claimed to be chaste –
        This last statement, however, needs checking.

Come to Flora's for wine and fine waters,
And for diddling in clean, classy quarters;
    I assure every guest,
    I've made personal test
Of my booze and my beds and my daughters!

Jack said to his wife: "Listen, Jill,
If you manage an orgasm, will
    You make sure I know?"
    She answered: "Right-ho!"
And she did, in a phone call from Rhyl.

JOHN SLIM

An amorous maiden, antique,
Kept a man in her house for a week;
    He entered her door
    With a thunderous roar,
But his exit was marked by a squeak!

There's a small Bed & Breakfast in Ryde,
Offers dominatrix on the side;
   Their advert should be:
   "S & M, B & B" –
There's a queue all around the outside.

A keen lassie who has to have cock,
Every hour, on the hour, round the clock,
   Cries: "Two, four, six, eight –
   Times three. I can't wait!"
And she keeps a spare tucked in her frock!

There was a young lady named Blunt,
Who had a rectangular cunt;
   She learned, for diversion,
   Posterior perversion,
Since no one could fit her in front.

There was a lascivious wench,
Whom nothing could ever make blench;
   She admitted men's poles
   At all possible holes,
And she'd bugger, fuck, jerk-off and French.

There was a young girl of Des Moines,
Whose cunt could be fitted with coins;
   Till a guy from Hoboken
   Inserted a token,
And now she rides free on the ferry.

A lap-dancing club is a place,
Where damsels, who've spurned social grace,
    Will strip off their gear,
    Stick a tit in your ear,
And waggle their bum in your face.

When the Duchess of Bagliofuente,
Took her fourteenth cavaliere servente,*
    The Duke said: "Old chappy
    I'll keep that quim happy,
If I have to hire nineteen or twenty."

* In eighteenth-century Italy, the acknowledged lover of a married woman.

Thank God for the Duchess of Gloucester,
She accommodates all who accost her;
    She will welcome the prick
    Of Tom, Harry, and Dick,
Or old Baldwin, and even Lord Astor.

Said a floosie called Susie: "Although
You have heard I'm a bird who will show
    A slick mix of tricks,
    With up to six dicks,
It ain't necessarily so!"

JOHN SLIM

No danger you might drop a clanger
With a tart who works cars at Stavanger;
   Although she extols
   A roll in a Rolls,
She still likes a bang in a banger!

     There was a young lady named Mabel
     Who would fuck on a bed or a table;
       Though a two-dollar screw
       Was the best she could do,
     Her behind bore a ten-dollar label.

A chippy whose name was O'Dare,
Sailed forth on a ship to Kenmare;
   But this cute little honey
   Had lost all her money,
So she laid the whole crew for her fare.

     Said a dainty young whore named Miss Meggs:
     "All the boys like to spread my two legs;
       Then slip in between,
       If you know what I mean,
     And deposit the whites of their eggs."

An eager young farm girl named Mabel
At milking was not all that able;
   But, to get the thing right,
   She would practise each night
With some sausages, under the table.

Any whore whose door sports a red light,
Knows a prick when she sees one, all right;
   She can tell by a glance,
   From the drape of men's pants,
If they're worth taking on for the night.

An innocent thing from Missouri
Quite fancied herself as a houri;
   Her friends sadly took her
   For a tart and forsook her,
So she gave up the role in a fury.

Said the tart: "From the start, to be blunt,
I thought the runt's stunt an affront –
   He asked me for credit!
   As soon as he said it,
I told him I liked it up front!"

        When asked: "Do you smoke while you screw?"
        A call girl said: "Maybe I do,
           If ever constriction
           Creates enough friction,
        Though I'm not in the best place to view!"

        JOHN SLIM

A generous chick from Pana,
Who fucked everyone, near and far;
   When asked to explain
   Simply said, with disdain:
"I am trying to save for a car."

        There were three naughty ladies of Fetters,
        Who outraged all their elders and betters
           They stuffed their cock-holders
           With notes from stockholders,
        Unpaid bills and anonymous letters.

There once was a girl from the chorus,
Whose virtue was known to be porous;
   She started by candling,
   And ended up handling
The whole clientele of a whorehouse.

In Brooklyn, New York, there's a lass
Who will hitch up her dress when you pass;
   If you toss her two bits,
    She will show you her tits,
And allow you to fondle her ass.

A feminist tart of great flair,
Had a system surprising and rare:
   Though meekly compliant
    With the needs of the client,
She insisted on paying her share!

JOHN SLIM

A hooker who worked in Black Buff,
Had a pussy as big as a muff;
   It had room for both hands,
   And some intimate glands,
And was soft as a little duck's fluff.

      There was a young lady named Mabel,
      Who would spreadeagle out on the table,
         And cry to her man:
         "Stuff in all that you can –
      Get your bollocks in too, if you're able!"

The hard-up young call girl was brash,
Explaining her marks with panache –
   She said to her mum:
   "I get thrashed on my bum,
'Cos that's what I am – strapped for cash!"

      A hooker, who's also a cook,
      Tried writing a prize-winning book;
         Said the cook who's a hooker:
         "I'll make my book Booker,
      If each judge, for an hour, books my nook!"

The eager first mate of a lugger,
Once took out a girl keen to hug her;
   "I've my monthlies," she said,
   "And a cold in the head,
But my bowels are fine – do you bugger?"

There was a young girl of Detroit
Who, at fucking, was very adroit;
   She could squeeze her vagina
   To a fine line, or finer,
And open it out like a quoit.

She had a good friend named Durand
Whose cock could contract or expand;
   He could diddle a midge,
   Or the arch of a bridge –
Their performance together was grand!

A delightful young girl from Darjeeling,
Although generous warm and appealing,
   Considers it rude,
   To be totally nude,
But her outfits are rather revealing!

LES WILKIE

There was a young lady in Bude
Who went for a swim in the nude;
   She cared not a jot
   For the catcalls she got –
Though she certainly wasn't a prude.

ELEANOR ROGERS

There is a young chap in South Park
Who, whenever he screws, has to bark;
  His wife is a bitch
  With a terrible itch,
So the town never sleeps after dark.

    There was a young harlot named Heather,
    Whose twitcher was not unlike leather;
      She attracted the boys,
      Simply making a noise
    As she flapped the two edges together.

    There was an old whore named McGhee,
    Who was first in the queue for a spree;
      Said she: "For a fuck,
      I charge half a buck,
    And I throw in the asshole for free!"

A worldy-wise gal from Des Moines,
Had a very large sackful of coins:
  The nickels and dimes
  She got from the times
That she'd cradled young boys in her loins.

There once was a floozie named Annie,
Whose prices were cosy, but canny:
  A buck for a fuck,
  Fifty cents for a suck,
And a dime for a feel of her fanny.

A delightful young Swedish au pair
Achieved introductions with flair:
    "Hello! I am Nordic!
    I simply adordic!
So pleased to meet you! Put it there!"

A promiscuous maiden from Chester
Advised the young man who'd undressed her:
    "I think you may find
    That it's more fun behind –
For the front is beginning to fester."

I once knew a harlot named Lou,
And a versatile girl she was, too;
   After ten years of whoredom,
   She perished of boredom,
And married a jackass. Yes – you!

A virgin who lives in Kentucky,
Admits: "I've been terribly lucky;
   No man ever, yet,
   On my back made me get,
Though I do sometimes feel awful fucky!"

There was a Hell's Kitchen Y. T.
Who said to two boyfriends: "Aw, gee,
   I don't think that coitus
   Could possibly hoit us!"
So they did it together, all three.

An unfortunate lady from Rhyl,
Felt the omnibus had made her ill;
   So she called the conductor,
   Who obligingly fucked her,
Which did her more good than a pill!

I love her in her evening gown,
I love her in her nightie.
   When moonlight flits
   Betwixt her tits –
Jesus Christ, almighty!

A naive young maiden of Bude,
Had never seen any man nude;
When a lewd fellow showed
All he had in the road,
She did not know quite what to conclude.

A fencing contractor did well,
To employ a young beauty named Nell;
She helped with the filing
And contract compiling,
And sometimes erections as well.

There is a young girl named O'Clare,
Whose body's all covered with hair;
It's really quite fun
To probe with one's gun –
For her pussy might be anywhere!

Lady Lust is an amorous soul,
Always hot for a substantial pole;
Her well-endowed chauffeur
She treats as her gopher,
And, boy, does he go for her hole!

One subversive young harlot, quite neat,
Was led to fifth-column deceit;
When the paratroops landed,
Her trade was expanded
By at once going down on their meat.

The chief charm of a whore in Shalott
Was the absence of hair on her twat;
   She kept it smooth-looking
   Not by shaving or plucking,
But by all the attention it got.

      There was a young lady of Andover,
      And the boys used to ask her to handover
         Her sexual favour,
         Which she did (may God save her!)
      For her morals she had no command over.

There was a young lady named Hicks
Who quite happily played with men's pricks,
   Which she always embellished
   With evident relish,
Until they stood up and did tricks.

      "A garden hose!" cried Mrs Biddle,
      And she ordered her husband: "Go fiddle!
         This is double the fun,
         And you get three in one –
      A good ducking, a douche, and a diddle!"

There was a young woman of Croft
Who played with herself in a loft,
   Having reasoned that candles
   Could never cause scandals,
Besides which they never went soft.

There was a young lady named May
Who strolled in a park by the way,
   She met a young man
    Who fucked her and ran –
Now she visits the park every day.

Said another young woman of Croft,
Amusing herself in the loft:
   "A salami or brockwurst
    Is what I should choose first –
With bologna you know you've been boffed!"

A prim young fellatrix named Prue,
Said: "There's one thing nice girls will not do:
  You may touch my rear end,
  But if my up-here end
Should appeal, there's a hole in that too!"

Dear Mummy, how can I begin
To tell you I'm living in sin,
  With Cyril, who's naughty,
  Quite bald, fat and forty,
And constantly plies me with gin?

JOHN SLIM

There was a young girl named Miss Randall,
Who thought it beneath her to handle
  A young fellow's pole,
  So instead, her hot hole
She contented by means of a candle.

A prudish young damsel named Rose,
Is particular how chaps propose;
  To "Let's have intercourse."
  She says, gaily: "Of course!"
But to "Let's fuck!" she turns up her nose.

A precocious young lady named Lee,
Once scrambled up into a tree,
  And when she got there,
  Her asshole was bare,
And so was her c-u-n-t.

There was a young lady named Rose,
Who'd occasionally straddle a hose,
    And cavort about, squirting
    And spouting and spurting,
Pretending she pissed like her beaux.

There was a young lass of Devizes,
Whose tits were of quite different sizes;
    The one on the right
    Was an eye-catching sight,
But the other three held no surprises.

JOHN SLIM

An inventive young girl named Maxine,
Found an interesting use for the bean;
   As a vaginal bearing,
   She found it hard-wearing,
And it varied her fucking routine.

There was a young lady named Rose,
With erogenous zones in her toes;
   She remained onanistic,
   Till a foot-fetishistic
Young man became one of her beaux.

A fair-haired young damsel named Grace,
Felt it really quite foolish to place
   Her hand on your cock,
   When it turned hard as rock,
For fear it would spit in her face!

There was a young girl of Mobile,
Whose hymen was fashioned from steel;
   To give her a thrill
   Took a rotary drill,
Or a Number 9 emery wheel.

The nipples of Lilly Lapsong,
When excited, grew twelve inches long;
   Embarrassed, her lover,
   Was shocked to discover,
She expected no less of his dong!

A young maiden who lives in Duluth,
Is a striver and seeker of truth;
    Such a pretty young wench,
    And so practised at French
She insists that all else is uncouth.

        There was an old tart, Goldilocks,
        Whose motto was: I Gobble Cocks.
            This frank declaration
            Brought such reputation,
        She spent years sucking cocks on the docks.

Young Sherry surrendered her cherry,
On the Fishguard to Rosslare fast ferry;
    She knew she'd been kissed
    In enveloping mist,
But, by which mister – Gerry or Terry?

        A bored laundry worker, from Lyme,
        Felt the job had no reason or rhyme,
            Till she found true elation
            With the spinner's vibration –
        Now she's put in for more overtime!

        CAROL ANNE DAVIS

There was a young lady named Mandel,
Who caused such a neighbourhood scandal,
    By dancing, quite bare,
    In the main village square,
Whilst frigging herself with a candle.

Said Susie: "I've never denied
That my breasts are quite frequently eyed;
   But I don't think their size is
   The cause of surprises –
It's having all four side by side!"

JOHN SLIM

Said a comely, sweet, red-headed siren:
   "These young sailors are cute – I must try one!"
      She came home in the nude,
      Stewed, screwed and tattooed
With lewd pictures and verses from Byron.

There was a young girl named Maxine,
Whose vagina was wondrously clean;
   She stayed safe from attack
   With her uterus packed
With a dill pickle, papulous, green.

       Have you heard of old Widow O'Reilly,
       Who regarded her husband so highly,
          That in spite of the scandal,
          Her umbrella handle
       Was made from his membrum virile.

There was a young lady of Wantage,
Of whom the Town Clerk took advantage;
   Said the County Surveyor:
   "Of course you must pay her –
You've altered the line of her frontage!"

       As his passenger stripped in North Wales,
       Gordon spotted the Police on their tails;
          He remarked: "Looks like fuzz,"
          She replied: "Yes, it does.
       But what were you expecting – pigtails?"
       DENNIS WALKER

She fashioned a thing of soft leather,
And embellished the end with a feather;
   When she poked it inside her,
   She soared like a glider,
And gave up her lover forever.

A lady who lives in Moncrieff,
Satisfies several men with relief:
    Wee Gregory Sunday,
    Big Fred every Monday,
And Tuesday to Saturday – Keith.

LES WILKIE

When a naturist stopped in a layby,
Thinking: 'Here's enough sun to make hay by',
    And a man in a truck
    Shouted: "Give us a fuck!"
She smiled: "Those aren't the rules that I play by."

Miss de Vaughan was a maker of panties,
For all from schoolgirls to grand-aunties;
    Her successful press ad
    Was herself, lightly clad,
In her reasonably-priced silky scanties.

Said a busy young whore known as Mabel,
Who at fucking was willingly able:
    "It's a pity to waste
    All that juicy white paste."
So she served it in bowls at the table.

A blushing young bride from Tonypandy,
Has discovered her quim is quite handy;
    On their wedding night,
    To the couple's delight,
She filled it with three pints of brandy.

A naked hitch-hiker is thumbing,
At the side of the road, looking stunning,
   With a sign that says BEDS –
   Quite enough to turn heads –
I can already feel myself coming...

An engaging young maiden, a honey,
Had a habit you may find quite funny:
   She would roll up a buck,
   In her pussy, to fuck,
So her husband would come into money.

If they sign themselves Mr & Mrs
Smith, then the likelihood this is
   A dirty weekend
   With a very good friend –
Well, let's hope they fulfil all their wishes!

There was a young lady from Gloucester
Whose friends were afraid they had lost her;
   Till they saw, on the grass,
   The imprint of her arse,
And the knees of the man who had crossed her.

Said cosmonaut Katie to Pete:
"They say we've been most indiscreet;
   But, hell's teeth, I'm burstin'
   With pride – we're the first in
The Ten-Light-Years-High-Club, my sweet!"

RON RUBIN

An adventurous maiden once said,
As her lover jumped into the bed:
   "I'm so tired of this stunt
   One performs with one's cunt,
Why not pop up my bottom instead!"

        Cries a popular whore named Miss Randalls,
        As one after another she handles:
           "When the work gets this busy,
           My cunt gets all jizzy,
        And it runs down my legs like wax candles."

        A whorehouse at 9 Rue de Rennes,
        Didn't seem to be luring the men,
           Till they got in some fairies
           With such pretty dilberries,
        That their clientele increased again.

Whilst riding without any pants,
On the back of a Harley in France,
   I got toots from a man
   In a Citroen Dyanne,
And a trucker from Watford, Northants.

In the hay in the barn in the yard,
The farmer told Susie from Chard:
   "Come here, pretty Sue,
   I've a soft spot for you."
She answered: "I'll wait till it's hard!"

JOHN SLIM

An insatiable lady from Dover,
Had unquenchable passion that drove her
   To cry (when you came):
   "Oh, gadzooks! What a shame!
I'm afraid we shall have to start over."

A forthright young maiden of Ealing,
Whose lover was before her, kneeling,
   Said: "Please, dearest Jim,
   Take your hand off my quim,
I would much prefer fucking to feeling."

ISAAC ASIMOV

       A clever young conjuror lass,
       Reclined with a chap in the grass;
          She performed quite a trick
          On the end of his dick,
       Till it foamed like a bottle of Bass.

Three insatiable siblings named Biddle,
Indulged in a three-cornered diddle;
   Though those on each side
   Were quite well satisfied,
All fought for dual joys in the middle.

       A lady with features cherubic,
       Was famed for her area pubic;
          When they asked her its size,
          She replied, in surprise:
       "Are you talking of square feet, or cubic?"

There was a young lady of Gwent,
With a cunt of enormous extent,
   And so deep and so wide
   The acoustics inside,
Were so good you could hear when you spent.

      In a greengrocer's shop in the region,
      A visiting sex-starved Glaswegian
         Saw a notice which read:
         Loose Swedes, so she said:
      "Give me two – and a naughty Norwegian!"

      JOHN SLIM

A tart who is targeting truckers,
Realizing they're all filthy fuckers,
   Imposes high tolls
   On each of her holes,
And makes a fortune from the suckers.

There once was a versatile whore,
As expert behind as before;
   For a quid you could view her,
   And bugger and screw her
As she stood on her head on the floor.

      A handsome young widow named Vi,
      Has seduced all the wardens nearby;
         When the sirens said: "Woo!"
         Well, what else could they do
      To extinguish the gleam in her eye?

A virgin with urges quite loose,
Thought; "I'll have to employ self-abuse!"
    She ran to the garden,
    In search of a hard-on,
And was had by a statue of Zeus.

An inventive old biddy of Troy,
Has devised a delightful new joy:
    She will sugar the rim,
    Of her quivering quim,
And then have it sucked off by a boy.

There was a young girl, very sweet,
Who found mariners' meat such a treat;
   When she sat on their laps
   And unbuttoned their flaps,
She would always find plenty to eat!

      An eager young maiden named Carter,
      Fell in love with a virile young Tartar;
         She ripped off her pants,
         Gave his prick a quick glance,
      And announced: "For that I'll be a martyr!"

      A talented fuckstress, Miss Chisholm,
      Was renowned for her fine paroxysm;
         While the chap detumesced,
         She still spent on with zest,
      Her rapture sheer anachronism.

No woman's been known to refuse,
To go with a friend to the loos,
   And line up in force,
   With handbags, of course,
While minding their pees and their queues.

JOHN SLIM

      A lascivious maiden whose mind,
      Was never especially refined,
         With a lover to please,
         Would drop to her knees,
      And he'd stick his prick in from behind.

A lift operator, Miss Brown,
Who has recently moved into town,
   Has had quite enough
   Of (ding!) going up,
And far prefers (dong!) going down!

       There were several young ladies of Grimsby
       Who said: "Of what use can our quims be?
          The hole in the middle
          Is so we can piddle,
       But for what can the hairs on the rims be?"

I don't mind if a girl rides a 'copter,
I don't mind if a girl rides a car,
   But the girl who rides astraddle
   An old fashioned saddle
Is stretching things a bit too far.

       There was a young lady named Nelly,
       Whose tits could be juggled like jelly;
          They could tickle her twat,
          Or be tied in a knot,
       And could even swat flies on her belly.

Curvaceous young ladies are full,
Of whiles and beguilement and bull;
   They manage this better
   Whilst wearing a sweater,
And pull your eyes over the wool!

The Duchess of Snood's crude and lewd,
And the men think her terribly rude,
    When they swim in the docks,
    She will tickle their cocks,
And guffaw when the red tips protrude!

        A talented tart, home-from-homely,
        Eager chaps won't allow to be lonely,
            Has to hang out in front
            Of her popular cunt
        A sign reading: Standing Room Only!

Bernadette was a beautiful whore,
Who wore sixty-six beads, nothing more.
    They sneered: "Unrefined!"
    When she wore them behind,
So, she thoughtfully wore them before.

        An ugly old spinster in France,
        Who all the men looked at askance,
            Threw her skirt overhead,
            And then jumped into bed,
        Shouting: "Now I've a *much* better chance!"

There was a young lady named Flo,
Whose lover had pulled out too slow;
    So they tried it all night,
    Till he got it just right –
Well, practice makes perfect you know!

There was a young lady with thighs
Which, when spread, showed a slit of such size
   (This deep and *that* wide),
   You could play cards inside –
Very much to her bridegroom's surprise.

A prick-teasing virgin from Bude,
Employs tricks which, though welcome, are viewed
   With confusion by chaps:
   Yes, she fondles their sacks,
But will never permit them intrude.

     An insatiable young fellatrix
     Was attending to five perky pricks;
        With a sudden loud cry,
        She whipped out her glass eye:
     "Tell the boys I'll accommodate six!"

A taxi-cab whore out of Iver,
Would do the round trip for a fiver;
   Quite reasonable, too,
   For a sight-see, a screw,
And a fifty-cents tip for the driver.

VICTOR GRAY

     A young student who taught in Devizes,
     Has appeared at the local assizes;
        She'd been teaching the boys
        Matrimonial joys,
     And had given French letters as prizes.

"Though a hardware store clerk," said Miss Hughes,
"There are some kinds of work I refuse;
   I will handle their nuts
   And their bolts and crosscuts,
But I'm buggered if I'll dish out screws!"

If you're mentioning actions immoral,
Then how about handing the laurel
      To doughty Queen Esther,
      No three men could best her –
One fore, and one aft, and one oral!

There was a young harlot from Kew,
Who filled her vagina with glue;
   She said, with a grin:
   "If they pay to get in,
They can pay to get out again too!"

A gentleman ought to show gratitude,
When a lady affords him some latitude,
      By adjusting her dress
      To permit a caress
And assuming a welcoming attitude.

A magnum or two of champagne,
Will go a long way to make plain,
      That his feelings are such,
      That he hopes very much,
She'll allow him to feel her again . . .

CYRIL RAY

In the shade of the old apple tree,
There between her fat legs I could see,
   A little brown spot
   With the hair in a knot,
And it certainly looked good to me.

I asked as I tickled her tit,
If she thought that my big thing would fit;
   She said it would do,
   So we had a fine screw
In the shade of the old apple tree.

In the shade of the old apple tree,
I got all that was coming to me;
   In the soft, dewy grass
   Such a beautiful ass
From a maiden delicious to see.

I could hear the dull buzz of a bee
As he sank his grub hooks into me;
   Her ass it was fine,
   But you should have seen mine
In the shade of the old apple tree!

       A lascivious hussy, from Ealing,
       Woke from sleep with a splendid new feeling:
          Not under the cover
          Alongside her lover
       But suspended by chains from the ceiling.

GEOFF HARRIS

And a similar one called Miss Dors;
Each renowned as a brassière filler,
    They seemed to defy Nature's laws.
    For the actress a "must"
    Is an oversized bust.
    You may think it is just
    An incitement to lust,
But with it her fate's to go sweeping the States,
When without she makes more sweeping floors.

AUSTIN BAKER

There was a young lady named Haste,
So determined to marry still chaste;
    But, whilst out on a ramble,
    She emerged from a bramble
Much dishevelled and very red-faced!

DENNIS WALKER

Eileen Backwards, at Paddington Station,
Met a chap whose intent was predation;
    She was moved to explain
    That, in spite of her name,
She did not have the least inclination!

PAMELA TRUDIE HODGE

Caesar thought Cleopatra was peachy,
And declared: "There's so much she could teach me!"
    When he mentioned new heights
    Of erotic delights
It was "veni", not "vidi" or "vici"!

JANET SMITH

When the census man called upon Gail,
Whose clients were all strictly male,
    And said: "Your career
    Should be written here."
She entered just one word: "Wholesale".

GEORGE McWILLIAM

There was a young girl of Trebarwith,
Whom a cad in a car went too far with,
    Which disproves a report
    That she wasn't the sort
For going too far in a car with.

RJP HEWISON

The last time I met Madam X,
(Ever keen to administer sex),
   She whipped me at will,
   Then presented her bill
Which read: "Plastic, or cash, but no cheques."

        When she jumped in the back of the car,
        And removed both her knickers and bra,
           I knew I would like her,
           This stunning hitchhiker,
        But warned her: "I'm not going far!"

An elderly tart admits: "Men!
I cannot have too many of them!"
   Though the front of her pants
   Lists her cans and her can'ts,
With a note: Best before 8 p.m!

        Although she looks fairly aloof,
        Nobody gives blow-jobs like Ruth;
           She'll envelop your knob
           In her sexy, young gob:
        Look, here, under this blanket – the proof!

A dissatisfied, bitter, old bitch,
Had a motorized self-frigger, which
   She employed with delight
   For the whole of the night –
Twenty bucks, Abercrombie & Fitch.

When a man in a van (it's a camper)
Announced: "I am going to Tampa."
   She approved the appeal
   Of a bloody good feel,
And said: "That's a plan I won't hamper!"

We go down to Dog Paddle Creek,
Skinny-dipping at least twice a week;
   Betty-Lou only swims
   With two pink waterwings,
And she don't seem to mind if we peek!

Her boobs have been fashioned from plastic,
And I must say they look quite fantastic;
   Though she will not confide
   Their true size, a rough guide
Is: they're tucked in her knicker elastic!

In the bar at the Lamb & Giraffe,
She whipped out her tits for a laff;
   For a coffee and bun
   She'd have shown you her bum –
Aren't you sorry you weren't down the caff?

Roll up, ladies! Why don't you fill those
Panting pussies with one of our dildos?
   A bonus is that
   With the batteries flat,
It may stutter and splutter but still goes!

I couldn't have been any greener,
The first time I fucked Wilhemina;
    Yes, she was my first,
    And she conjured a wurst
Out of what was no more than a wiener!

        Pert nipples like sweet nectarines,
        A cute arse clad in skimpy blue jeans;
            She gives such slick blow-jobs
            To Tom, Dick, and Joe Bloggs –
        But she's only the girl of their dreams!

A lady from Leeds who's expressed
A need to be known as the best
    In bed, on the job,
    Whatever the knob,
Accommodates any request!

JOHN SLIM

        There was a young lady from Cheam,
        Who filled up her bath with ice cream;
            When some time had gone by,
            She gave vent to a cry
        And proceeded to lick herself clean.

A lady of Leck is lamenting,
The shortage of men that's preventing,
    The sounds of the stuffing
    And huffing and puffing,
That signify adults consenting.

A lady – by nature quite dour,
Liked to stand on her hands in the shower;
    There, with quivering sighs,
    She would open her thighs
And remain thus for over an hour.

Said a lady who'd strayed in Kincaid:
"It's not down to me, I'm afraid,
    If Fate takes the view
    That I'm due for a screw,
Well – whatever I do, I get laid!"

"I shall nurture my 48D,
And appear in the Sun on page three;
    I'll be tickled to bits
    If lads ogle my tits!"
Sounds like naked ambition to me.

A tart who was new to the game,
Soon established considerable fame
    Using marketing tricks:
    Two-for-one for some pricks,
And a discount old codgers could claim!

There was an old whore in Flin Flon,
With a cleft like a barn. He got on
    And sensed something odd
    Straight away, the poor sod,
And after that, there he was – gone!

JOHN SLIM

In the street, a big lady from Fareham,
Would take out her tits to compare 'em;
    She explained: "As I'm blessed
    With great mounds on my chest,
It's a bit of a shame not to share 'em!"

A beginner who'd gone with a tart
Realized he'd no clue where to start;
    Till she guided his mitts
    To her interesting bits,
And soon helped him to master the art!

A lady who lived in Great Barr,
Considered her toy-boy a star:
"He can't keep his hands
Off my mammary glands –
So I use him instead of a bra!"

JOHN SLIM

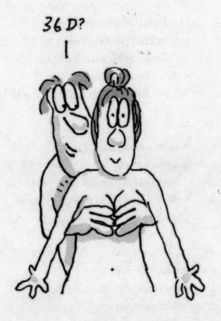

There was a young girl of Uttoxeter,
So ugly that men would throw rocks at her;
But her beautiful cousin
Drew men by the dozen,
And even had chaps flash their cocks at her.

RON RUBIN

A pneumatic young thing in Devizes,
Gives motor mechanics surprises:
   They don't use a jack –
   If she's flat on her back
Underneath, and breathes in, the car rises!

JOHN SLIM

"I admit I'm a bit of a tart,"
Says a Hollywood starlet, with heart;
   "That's why what I need
   Is a masculine lead
Who'll allow me to build up *his* part!"

A lady, considered a prude,
Slipped her clothes off and swam in the nude;
   Swimmers viewed to her waist
   Which seemed perfectly chaste,
Though, as divers, we cannot collude!

There was a young lady of Bicester
Who played sexual games with her sicester,
   As well as her brother,
   Her father and mother,
And when she left home, how they micester!

Said a baffled young bimbo of Brent:
"It was strange, to a certain extent –
   He was biting my bum,
   And I thought he might come,
But then he said 'Thank you!' and went."

A whore among oars in old Bewdley,
Enjoyed the coxed-fours rather crudely:
   Did a blow-job for two,
   Then invited a screw,
And the four, with their cox, lined up lewdly.

JOHN SLIM

      There was a plump lass, called Louisa,
      And all of the girls used to tease her;
         But some of the lads,
         And some of their dads
      Thought it more fun to fondle and squeeze her!

      RON RUBIN

A young window-dresser, called Kay,
Would not let herself go astray;
   Though many men tried,
   She always replied:
"These goods are just meant for display!"

ELEANOR ROGERS

      A much-diddled dolly named Beverley,
      Organizes her sex-life so cleverly;
         She services three
         At a time – all for free –
      Positioned about herself severally!

A well-travelled floozie of Ealing,
Has been screwed from New York to Darjeeling;
   You could say that she's been,
   From the age of sixteen,
Familiar with many a ceiling . . .

RON RUBIN

That crack
needs filling

A lady of Launceston who led
A life of debauchery, said:
   "All men are the same,
   Apart from their name,
Which I ask as they get out of bed!"

JOHN SLIM

A starry-eyed starlet named Charlotte,
Announced: "Hollywood! Home of the harlot!
   Where cute, split-tailed bitches
   Take quick rides to riches,
If their sins are sufficiently scarlet!"

      When ladies were laid in Kincaid,
      You could tell by the noises they made,
         They were happy with what
         Had been shot in their slot,
      And the very fair price they had paid.

There was an old madam in Cheltenham,
Who said: "Cunts? Why, of course dear, I've dealt in 'em,
   And I thought it my duty
   To make 'em so fruity
My clients used simply to melt in 'em!"

      A harlot from old Amarillo,
      Tired of finding strange heads on her pillow,
         Decided, one day,
         That to keep them at bay,
      She would plug up her pussy with Brillo.

Said Brenda, a bit of a dish:
"Though sixty-nine's fine, I just wish
   The fellows who play
   Wouldn't bob up and say
They're going, and thanks for the fish!"

A reluctant young lady of Wheeling
Had professed to lack sexual feeling,
   Till a bounder named Boris
   Barely brushed her clitoris,
And she had to be scraped off the ceiling.

     A brassy young lass attracts stares,
     For what her decolletage bares;
        It's one in the eye
        For the modest and shy,
     Well, two to speak true – but who cares?

"Succumb to your filthy desires?"
"I think not!" cried the haughty Miss Myers,
   "The only thing free
   That this part does is pee –
For the other, I've plenty of buyers!"

There's a sweet signorita, Cervantes,
Who will drive a lad mad in her scanties;
   She moves them to prose,
   And the pros, as she knows,
Day by day quite outweigh the few antis.

JOHN SLIM

     A candid young lady named Tudor,
     Remarked to the chap who'd just screwed her:
        "After dildos, dilators,
        And electric vibrators,
     The real thing feels like an intruder!"

A gentleman, dining in Bude,
Complained to the waitress: "You're rude!"
   She replied: "Wait and see
   Just how rude I can be!"
And she served him his soup in the nude.

RON RUBIN

There's a nympho who makes no pretext,
Of claiming to be undersexed;
   While she humps, what is heard
   Is a four-letter word –
Halfway through any screw, she shouts: "Next!"

JOHN SLIM

Old Nora still knows how to please,
Though she's knocking on ninety (the tease!);
    And when she feels flighty,
    Her flannelette nightie
Makes strong men go weak at the knees!

There was a young lady of Bicester,
Who was nicer by far than her sister;
    The sister would giggle,
    And wiggle and jiggle,
But this one would come if you kissed her!

A voracious young girl, from Red Hook,
Speculated: "I could be mistook,
    But one more time just
    About qualifies us
For that Guinness's World Record Book!"

There was a young lady called Kate,
Who rang up her beau for a date:
    "Let's make love at one,
    My sweet honey bun –
But start on your own if I'm late!"

RON RUBIN

Said an old maiden aunt: "My nirvana
Is based on the pleasures I garner:
    I always begin
    With a bottle of gin,
Two grapes and a token banana!"

JOHN SLIM

With her maidenhead gone with the wind,
Cried delirious ex-virgin Lucind:
    "It comes as a shock
    That I've missed so much cock –
That thing sure has a darn candle skinned!"

To her young virgin friend said Miss James:
"Sex is the most joyous of games!
    For what's pointed at you
    Ain't like on a statue,
You see: where marble dangles, meat aims!"

It occurred when she crossed the Atlantic,
But the fuck made young Yola quite frantic:
    It's not losing her cherry
    That upset her, not very –
But the aisle of a plane's unromantic!

A virtuous virgin of Thame,
Had resolved to live free of all shame;
    She wore four pairs of drawers,
    And of petticoats – scores,
But was screwed in the end, just the same.

There's a pert little flirt who's provoking,
The lads all the time by invoking
   Her right to a stuff
   Up the rough of her muff –
Then telling them all she was joking!

JOHN SLIM

On a blind date, flirtatious Miss Rowe,
When asked for a fuck, answered: "No!
   You may go second-class
   (Shove your prick up my ass),
But I'm saving my cunt for my beau."

An unfortunate maiden was Esther,
A peculiar repugnance possessed her;
   A reaction compulsive
   Made kissing repulsive,
Which was tough on all those who caressed her.

That sexy, posh tart you've just met –
You won't get your leg over yet;
   Forget fornication.
   You're joking! Fellation?
A hand-job's the best that you'll get!

Dildo prices, increasingly steep,
Have made many a broke girlie weep;
   In recession, the trend
   Is to make-do and mend,
And bananas, thank goodness, are cheap!

CAROL ANNE DAVIS

There was a young girl from Aberystwyth,
Who took grain to the mill to make grist with;
   The miller's son, Jack,
   Laid her on her back,
And united the organs they pissed with.

ALGERNON CHARLES SWINBURNE

She's had quite enough, you want more:
You must whisper to her: "*Je t'adore!*"
   Such pronouncements will win her,
   Then, once you are in her,
She'll soon be demanding: "*Encore!*"

An innocent lady from Woking,
Discovered she'd been quite provoking;
   But she thought it was grand
   When a gland made a stand
Quite unplanned on the strength of some stroking!

JOHN SLIM

In a dream an old brummie from Greet,
Was screwed in the nude in New Street,
   But the best of the joke
   Was when she awoke
And found mud on her bum and her feet!

There was an old madam called Rainey,
Adept at her business, and brainy;
   She charged forty bucks for
   An experienced whore,
And a five-dollar bill for a trainee.

An enormously fat girl, Regina,
Employed a young water-diviner
   To play a slick trick,
   With his prick as a stick,
To help relocate her vagina.

When supping some *vin ordinaire*,
She'd soon supped enough to declare:
   "This makes me want man
   As only *vin* can –
So who will oblige me, and where?"

There is a young lady named Mandy,
Whose right tit holds beer, which is handy
   If you wanted a drink –
   All the more when you think
Her left's lemonade for a shandy.

JOHN SLIM

A young maiden of English nativity,
Had a fanny of rare sensitivity;
    She could sit on the lap
    Of a Nazi or Jap,
And detect his Fifth Column activity.

A nymphomaniacal WAAC
Possessed a libidinous knack;
   Her erotic resources
   So pleased the armed forces,
She spent the whole war on her back.

There was a young lady called Tess,
Who went to a ball, in a dress;
    But the cut was so low
    That her boobs were on show –
I did have a quick look, I confess!

The seductive Dolores could lay so
Well, she earned many a peso
   From men who walked miles
   To climax with smiles –
Her ads in the papers all say so!

There was a punctilious bride
Who declared: "I have had to decide
   To walk up the knave –
   That's the central enclave –
Not the aisle (that's a bit on the side)."

JOHN SLIM

There was a young fellow named Adam
Whose mother had once been a Madam;
   As for Daddy, the score
   Was at least seven, for
On the day of conception, Ma'd had 'em!

The bottom of Elspeth McEagle
Is pink, plump, and perfectly regal;
   And when she bends low,
   And her ring is on show,
I have thoughts I believe are now legal.

CORNELIUS DOYLE

What he asked for (a four-letter word),
Badly frightened the virgin Miss Byrd;
   London Gin and insistence
   Soon wore down her resistance –
And the four-letter word then occurred.

A bikini-clad maiden in Bude,
Wondered: "Why are the men quite so rude?
   When I bathe in the sea,
   They will all follow me
In the hope that my boobs will protrude!"

The Queen of Old Egypt, named Cleo,
Conducted her loving *con brio*
   She felt quite at home in
   The arms of one Roman,
But preferred to be part of a trio.

There was a young girl from Penzance,
Who had clearly forgotten her pants
   Under such a thin dress
   (off-the-peg, M&S),
That's why all the lads asked her to dance.

There was a young lady called Claire,
Who streaked in the park for a dare;
   And all those who saw
   Could not agree more
That she had a magnificent pair!

The bride told the best man: "We'll share
A quick bit of nooky somewhere.
   You're here as the best,
   So I'd like a small test
To give me a chance to compare!"

The climax when Josie engages,
Is postponed for what seems to be ages;
   Out of self-preservation,
   And to banish frustration,
She has three or four fellows – in stages!

A pretty young harlot, in court,
Told the bench: "I'm less poor than you thought."
   Then lowered her drawers,
   To a round of applause,
And showed off her means of support!

Said Queen Isabella of Spain:
"I do like it now and again;
   But I wish to explain
   That by 'now and again'
I mean now, and again and again!"

As the elevator left our floor,
Poor Corinne caught her tits in the door;
   Though she yelled a great deal,
   Had those boobies been real
She'd have hollered considerably more!

There was a young woman named Maud,
Who found herself, now and then, floored,
   Or bedded, or chaired,
   Or top-of-the-staired –
Oh, well – that's the life of a bawd!

Young Alice is known for her poise
During quiet foreplay with the boys;
   But then, when she has 'em,
   At the brink of orgasm,
You can't hear yourself think for the noise!

         A virginal maiden named Kate,
         Who'd necked in the dark with her date,
            Was asked how she'd fared,
            And admitted though scared
         She was otherwise doing first-rate!

Gushed a lush in a seaside resort,
Drinking gin every night by the quart:
   "No mixers for me –
   I'm sure you can shee:
It'sh the gin that'sh the tonic, old shport!"

JOHN SLIM

Widow (conscious that time's on the wing),
Fortyish, but still game for a fling,
   Seeks fun-loving male,
   Mature, but not stale,
With a view to the usual thing.

SJ SHARPLESS

Shirley's face is all careworn and ashen,
The result of insatiable passion;
   Though she knows it's not right,
   She screws hard, day and night,
Just in case it should go out of fashion.

Thanks to sex a young woman named Carol,
Looked delightful in model's apparel;
    The slimming effect
    Was best, I suspect,
When her man had her over a barrel!

ISAAC ASIMOV

Have you come across Foo-Foo la Rue,
She who thinks it delightful to screw?
    Although not particular,
    She prefers perpendicular –
A talent known only to few!

When Jane and young Marcus first fiddled,
At school, she cried out: "I've been diddled!"
    For she found he'd a cock,
    Whilst, under her frock,
She had only the hole where she tiddled!

During screwing a strumpet from Woking,
Reacted so much to the poking,
    Her gyratory motion
    Caused such heat and commotion,
That her pussy and pubes started smoking!

There was a young woman named Melanie,
Who was asked by a man: "Do you sell any?"
    She replied: "No, siree!
    I give it for free –
To sell it, dear sir, is a felony!"

ISAAC ASIMOV

My dear, you look simply divine,
And I know that we'll get along fine;
    For making ends meet
    Will be such a treat,
When one end is yours, and one mine.

An insatiable strumpet, named Annie,
Had fleas, lice, and crabs in her fanny;
    Getting into her flue?
    Like a trip to the Zoo –
Wild beasts lurked in each nook and cranny.

There was a young chap of high station,
Who was found by a pious relation
    Having sex in a ditch
    With – I won't say a bitch –
But a lady of scant reputation!

On the boobs of a barmaid in Sale,
Are tattooed all the prices of ale;
    And, on her behind,
    For the sake of the blind,
Is the same list of prices in Braille.

My landlady frigs every night,
Which gives her a deal of delight;
    At my peephole I watch
    For a glimpse of her crotch,
But she usually puts out the light.

CORNELIUS DOYLE

There's a bimbo who's anxious to score
With such style that it's hard to ignore –
   There's one way she likes:
   On the crossbars of bikes,
On her back, going up the A4.

A notorious harlot, named Hearst,
In the pleasures of men is well-versed;
   Reads a sign at the head
   Of her well-rumpled bed:
"The client must always come first."

In her youth, exhibitionist Annie
Was frequently spanked by her nanny;
   That is why, to this day,
   Some psychiatrists say
She is fond of exposing her fanny!

ISAAC ASIMOV

Said a woman, with open delight:
"My pubic hair's perfectly white!
   I admit there's a glare,
    But the fellows don't care –
They locate it more quickly at night!"

ISAAC ASIMOV

There was a young lady named Maude,
A sort of society fraud;
   In the parlour, 'tis told,
   She was distant, quite cold,
But on the verandah, my gawd!

Said a strumpet, from Newton-le-Willows,
Whilst arranging two plump, feather pillows
   Beneath her trim bum:
   "Sex is sinful to some,
But to me men are mere peckerdillos!"

A determined young lady of taste,
Liked to keep herself virgin and chaste,
   And stoutly defended
   With gin traps suspended
On filigree chains from her waist!

A lass of curvaceous physique,
Preferred dresses that made her look chic;
   But all would agree
   That topless to knee
Did little to help her mystique.

DOUGLAS CATLEY

The muff-diving champ of St Ives,
Used to practise on other chaps' wives,
    Till a Mrs de Pole
    Simply swallowed him whole –
An experience we'll hope he survives.

CORNELIUS DOYLE

A certain young fellow, named Vaughan,
Once felt irresistibly drawn
    To exhibit in fun
    That involved more than one
So he screwed his best girl on the lawn.

ISAAC ASIMOV

A voluptuous dancer, from Wheeling,
Always danced with such exquisite feeling;
    There was never a sound,
    For miles around,
Save for fly-buttons hitting the ceiling!

Another young woman, named Claire,
Always walks around perfectly bare,
    Saying: "All that I show
    Are my publics, you know,
For my privates are covered with hair."

ISAAC ASIMOV

A harlot most gorgeously stacked,
Believed screwing a glorious act;
   And providing a niche
   For those who were rich
Saw her diamonded, minked, and Cadillaced.

       There was a young lady of Louth,
       Who'd returned from a trip to the South;
          Her father said: "Nelly,
          There's more in your belly
       Than ever went in by your mouth!"

A greedy seed merchant from Goring,
Insisted his wife should go whoring;
   And, I shall put it in writing,
   Though he found it exciting,
She found it exceedingly boring.

       Some gels, and I don't understand 'em,
       Will strip off their garments at random,
          Without any qualms,
          To exhibit their charms –
       In short: *quod erat demonstrandum!*

There was a young girl from Fort Kent
Who said that she knew what it meant
   When men asked her to dine,
   Gave her roses and wine –
She knew what it meant, but she went!

An innocent damsel named Grace,
Deemed it truly unseemly to place
   One's hand on a cock
   That might turn hard as rock
And, quite likely, explode in one's face!

There is a young girl in Virginia
Whose figure's alarmingly linear;
   Her vital statistics
   Resemble a dipstick's –
The truth is, she couldn't be skinnier!

"I am just," moaned a girl from Racine,
A perpetual motion machine;
   I can't help it, I must,
   For I service the lust
Of a sex-starved young US Marine."

ISAAC ASIMOV

3.
The Seamier Side of Academia, including a Student of Cambridge Named Hunt

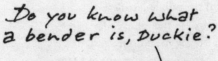

A randy professor, named Bert,
Was attracted to every new skirt;
   And it wasn't their minds
   But their rounded behinds
That excited this naughty old flirt.

      The unfortunate Dean of South Herts,
      Was caught importuning some tarts;
         His good wife was shocked
         When the Dean was unfrocked –
      For the first time she saw all his parts!

There was a young student of Queens,
Who haunted the public latrines;
   He was heard, in the john,
   Shouting: "Bring me a don!
But please, spare me those dreary old deans."

      There was a young lady called Burton,
      Who outraged other fellows at Girton,
         By cycling to town
         Without wearing a gown,
      And, what's worse, without even a skirt on!

There once was a fellow of Wadham,
Who approved of the folk ways of Sodom;
   "For a man might," he said,
   "Have a very poor head,
And yet be a fine fellow, at bottom."

An infamous student named Jones,
Would reduce any maiden to moans,
   With his wonderful knowledge
   (Acquired at college)
Of nineteen erogenous zones!

A giddy young girl up at Girton,
When found out of bounds with no skirt on,
   Explained to her tutor:
   "I thought it looked cuter –
A subject I'm quite an expert on!"

A young choral scholar at King's,
Looked just like an angel, sans wings;
   But he had a proclivity
   For amorous activity,
And other un-angelic things!

Ethnologists, up with the Sioux,
Wired home for "two punts, one canoe".
   The answer, next day,
   Said: "Girls on the way,
But, what in hell's name's a panoe?"

Consistent disciples of Marx,
Will have to employ special narks,
    If nationalization
    Of all copulation
Leads to laissez-faire fucking in parks.

According to old Sigmund Freud:
Life is seldom so fully enjoyed
    As in human coition
    (In any position)
With the usual organs employed.

A geneticist living in Rheims,
In attempting to learn what life means,
    Has discovered the zip
    On a sizeable dick,
And insists that it's all in the jeans!

There once was a Cambridge BA,
Who pondered the problem all day,
    Of what there would be
    If c-u-n-t
Were divided by c-o-c-k.

A progressive professor named Winners,
Held a class every evening for sinners;
   They were graded and spaced
   So the very debased
Would not be held back by beginners.

An ailing old college Professor,
Met a worse-for-wear whore from Odessa;
   She applied all her arts
   To his genital parts,
But they only grew lesser and lesser.

There was an old phoney named Kinsey,
Whose ideas of fucking were flimsy;
   He knew how to measure
   A penis for pleasure,
But he came much too quick in a quim, see?

A lonely young student of Eton,
Used always to sleep with the heat on;
   Till he met a sweet lass,
   Who proffered her neat ass –
Now they slumber with only a sheet on.

A geneticist living in Delft,
Scientifically played with himself;
   And when he was done,
   He labelled it: SON,
And filed it away on a shelf.

      A zoologist's daughter in Ewing,
      Gave birth to a thing that keeps cooing;
         Said her father: "Now, Flo,
         What I'd so like to know,
      Isn't whether but what you've been screwing!"

A potty professor, named Dell,
Understood psychophysics so well;
   So much so when he shit,
   He would analyse it –
For its length, and its breadth, and its smell.

      Have you heard of Professor MacKay,
      Who beds all the young girls in the hay?
         Though he thinks it's romantic,
         He drives them all frantic
      By talking a wonderful lay!

The mathematician Von Blecks,
Has devised an equation for sex;
   Having proved a good fuck
   Isn't patience or luck,
But a function – of y over x.

There was a young student named Poole,
Who attended a library school;
   As he thumbed the index,
   All his thoughts turned to sex,
And his blood all ran into his tool.

There is an old Countess of Bray,
And you may find it odd when I say
   That in spite of her station,
   Rank, and education,
She always spells "cunt" with a "k".

      The ancient orthographer Chisholm,
      Caused a lexicographical schism;
         He wondered which letter
         Would suit the word better –
      A "g" or a "j" to spell "jism"?

Undergraduates, out on a spree,
Met a prostitute game for nooky;
   They requested they mount
   For a student discount,
So she offered: "Buy one, get one free!"

      The French teacher criticized Fran:
      "You're not doing as well as you can."
         With a gleam in her eyes
         She unbuttoned his flies,
      And sailed through her oral exam!

Small wonder the French Mistress hates,
That randy philanderer Bates;
   He's only to see
   The pin-up on page three,
And young Master Bates masturbates.

An old archaeologist, Throstle,
Has discovered a fabulous fossil;
   He knows, from its bend,
   And the knob at the end,
It's the peter of Paul the Apostle.

A facetious old Don of Divinity,
Boasted loudly his daughter's virginity:
   "They must have been dawdling
   Down at old Magdalen –
It wouldn't have happened at Trinity!"

A luscious young student, at Vassar,
Was hailed as a top-of-the-classer;
   But not in her studies,
   You old fuddy-duddies,
For she shone as a great piece-of-asser!

ISAAC ASIMOV

A professor of Latin, in London,
Feared females so much that he shunned 'em;
  While his sex-drive urged: "Go!"
  He insisted: "No, no –
Illegitimi non carborundum!"*

Don't let the bastards get you down.

A mathematician named Hall,
Has a hexahedronical ball;
   The cube of its weight
   Times his pecker, plus eight,
Is his phone number – give him a call!

A Peterhouse chap, sweet and tender,
Went out with two dons on a bender;
   After several days,
   He returned in a haze,
No longer so sure of his gender!

A confirmed multilinguist, I fear,
Finds conditions for flirting severe;
   A girl scarcely knows
   The response to a beau's:
"Bitte couchez avec mich, my dear?"

A student of Cambridge, named Hunt,
Entertaining his girl in a punt,
    Heard her say: "On the whole,
    While you're wielding that pole,
I'd prefer you avoided my front!"

Uninhibited student, young Marge,
Plunged into the Thames from a barge;
    Then a don, from a punt,
    Introduced up her cunt
An organ amazingly large.

There's a fellow in Abergavenny,
With French words, but not very many;
    This emerges, you see,
    When he says that *tant pis*
Means Aunty is spending a penny!

A naughty young schoolboy named Sonny,
Had discovered the thrill of his dummy,
    With a smile like a fool,
    He enjoyed pocket pool
Till his pants got all sticky and runny.

A young engineer named Moore,
Who, while not exactly a whore,
   Couldn't pass up a chance
   To take down her pants,
And compare some chap's stroke with her bore.

There is an anthologist who,
Has decided that naught is taboo;
   Her words are so rude,
   And her verses so lewd,
I am sure they'll appeal to you!

A randy professor, from Splott,
Used his tongue on the ladies a lot:
   "It's frustrating," cried he,
   "I know my ABC,
But can't find that elusive G-spot!"

CAROL ANNE DAVIS

4.

A Young Woman
Named Mame, a Tough Football
Game, and Other Sporting Lore

A cheerful young golfer, named Jock,
Gave his ball a three-hundred-yard sock;
   It doesn't sound far
   For a chap who shoots par,
But twas done with the end of his cock!

     A flighty type, hopeless at tennis,
     But at swimming and diving a menace,
       Took pains to explain:
       "It depends how you train –
     I was a streetwalker in Venice!"

Want some
fun, dearie?

Old Man Winter is here with his grouch;
It's that time when you sneeze and you slouch;
   Though you can't take your women
   Canoeing or swimming,
There's a lot to be said for the couch!

     A horse-racing follower, Cookie,
     Who enjoyed mixing gambling with nookie,
        Spent hours at her place,
        Before every race,
     Curled up with a likeable bookie.

Along windy rivers in Hunts,
Young couples make love in their punts;
   Beneath weeping willows,
   They lie on their pillows,
And murmur their gratified grunts.

     A young polo player, from Berkeley,
     Made love to his sweetheart berserkeley;
        In the midst of each chukka,
        He would break off and fuck her,
     Horizontally, laterally, verkeley!

After lunch, the old Duchess of Beck,
Thus announced: "If you'll listen one sec,
    We have found a chap's tool
    In the small swimming pool,
So would all of you gentlemen check?"

A Pole, with a pole in a punt,
Examined his lady-friend's front;
    But, whilst trying his luck,
    His long pole got stuck,
And unable to shove or to shunt!

GERDA MAYER

When the tennis ball soared high above,
Nellie rose to receive like a dove;
   But her leap in the air
   Caused her knickers to tear,
And her partner to cry out: "That's love!"

A team playing baseball in Dallas,
Called the umpire a shit out of malice;
   While this worthy had fits,
   The team made eight hits,
And a girl in the bleachers named Alice.

An athletic young fellow in Venice,
Got the stone from much straining at tennis;
   When his cock wouldn't stand,
   She who had it in hand,
Said: "These outdoor pursuits are a menace!"

A golfer named Sandy McFarr,
Went to bed with a Hollywood star;
   When he witnessed her gash, he
   Cried: "Quick! Get my mashie!
I'm convinced I can make this in par!"

A sexual athlete named Lyle,
Admits jogging just isn't his style;
  "I workout," he's said,
  "At home, in my bed –
Yes, a miss is as good as a mile!"

But not the way he does it

A fanatic gun-lover named Rust,
Was perverse to the point of disgust;
  His idea of a peach
  Had a sixteen-inch breech
And a pearl-handled forty-four bust.

With a mixed-doubles lady from Wall,
Her chest is what umpires recall;
    She serves and it swings
    And is called many things –
Double-fault the least likely of all!

JOHN SLIM

A swimmer with no legs, from Wick,
Swam the Channel stark-naked, quite quick,
    Expecting encores
    And praise and applause –
Instead people cried: "Clever dick!"

"Far more precious to me than my treasure,"
The old heiress announced, "Is my leisure;
    I am happy to screw
    The entire Harvard crew –
They are slow, but that lengthens the pleasure!"

An anxious young fellow named Sean
Always looked rather worried and worn;
    His girl, we suspect,
    Used to get him erect,
Then use him for quoits on the lawn!

Said a naturist golfer from Tring:
"In the rough in the buff is the thing;
    One never recalls
    Such accessible balls,
Nor quite so much freedom of swing!"

JOHN SLIM

Some naturists, camping near Wick,
Established a communal trick:
    One lay on the ground
    And rapidly found
The others played quoits with his dick.

JOHN SLIM

Gasped a golfer in old Donegal:
"You have sex twice a week, is that all?"
    "It isn't a lot," said his partner,
    "So what?
I'm a priest, and the parish is small."

Three whores took on nine men at once,
In their arseholes, their mouths, and their cunts;
    On golf fairways or green
    Are more typically seen
Eighteen balls and nine holes at such stunts.

A flighty type, hopeless at tennis,
But at swimming and diving a menace,
    Took pains to explain:
    "It depends how you train –
I was a streetwalker in Venice!"

A lady, an expert on skis,
Went out with a man who said: "Please,
    On the next precipice,
    Will you give me a kiss?"
She said: "Quick, before somebody sees!"

        Ornithologists, through their field-glasses,
        May observe frequent heaving bare arses;
            Thereby you'll understand
            Why, throughout this fair land,
        Such bird-watching appears to the masses.

A certain young woman named Mame,
Longs to play in a tough football game;
    You would think that can't be
    Since she's female, you see,
Yet she's making the team just the same!

There once was a member of Mensa,
Who was a most excellent fencer;
   The sword that he used
   Was his (line is refused,
And has now been removed by the censor).

A burly shot-hurler called Helen,
Had breasts each the size of a melon;
   They were large it is true,
   And her pussy was too –
Like a bifocal, full-colour aerial view
Of Cape Horn and the Straits of Magellan.

He accepted that both balls were out,
(Though he'd challenged the line-judge's shout),
   When he felt the strong draft
   In his shorts, fore and aft,
And realized what the fuss was about!

The *derrière* Doris displays
In the park never fails to amaze;
   She bounces and flounces
   Those wonderful ounces,
And old men are ecstatic for days.

She thought she was safe in that pool,
Swimming naked to keep herself cool;
    But she got such a shock
    When around a large rock
Came three farm lads, polite as a rule . . .

The new ladies' captain, Miss Duff,
Has a lovely, luxuriant muff;
    In his haste to get in her,
    One eager beginner
Lost both of his balls in the rough.

"Though I've had sex before a big fight,
My performance has always been right,"
    Said the boxer, "Oh, yes –
    The fight's been a mess,
But the sex has been right on the night."

JOHN SLIM

Tina's tennis has earned her renown,
With a smash that's the talk of the town;
    Her free-flowing chest
    Is seen at its best
Going up when she's on her way down!

A golfer who drives with some force,
Played a round at the Nudist Camp course;
    On losing control
    Of his shot he was told:
"It's goodbye to one's balls in this gorse!"

An inventive young swimmer is grinning,
Having worked out a new way of swimming;
   By a marvellous trick,
   He will scull with his prick,
Which attracts wild applause from the women.

5.
The Duchess of Riva, her Golden Retriever and Other Animals

An Argentine gaucho named Bruno,
Once said: "There is one thing I do know:
  A woman is fine,
  And the sheep are divine,
But a llama is Numero Uno!"

Most gauchos are only after one thing, but you're not like the others

An adventurous chap, from Bombay,
Took a slow boat to China one day,
  But was lashed to the tiller
  With a sex-starved gorilla –
And (yes) China's a fucking long way!

MARK BUMFORD

An unusual lady called Grace,
Had her eyes in a very strange place;
    She could sit on the hole
    Of a mouse or a mole,
And stare the poor beast in the face!

A keeper who's fucked quite a few
Chimpanzees and the odd kangaroo,
    Performs, just for laughs,
    Oral sex on giraffes –
Is no quadruped safe at the zoo?

A duchess who thought sex a treat,
Felt a gang-bang would make life complete;
    Fifteen dicks, and a dog,
    Promptly went the whole hog –
And the lady admitted defeat.

There once was a fellow called Zeigel
Who'd decided to bugger a beagle;
    And, just as he came,
    A voice, calling his name,
Said: "My turn, but you know it's illegal!"

In spite of a fearsome disease,
Lord Reilly gets down on his knees
    Before altars of Gods,
    Whores, lads and large dogs,
And all for such very small fees.

A habit obscene and unsavoury,
Holds the Bishop of Wessex in slavery:
    With maniacal howls,
    He deflowers young owls
Which he keeps in an underground aviary.

There was an old Scot, named McTavish,
Who attempted an anthropoid ravish;
    The object of rape
    Was the wrong sex of ape,
And the anthropoid ravished McTavish.

There was a young peasant named Gorse,
Who fell madly in love with his horse;
    Said his wife: "You rapscallion,
    That horse is a stallion –
This must constitute grounds for divorce!"

Concerning the bees and the flowers,
In the fields and the gardens and bowers,
    You will note, at a glance,
    That their ways of romance
Haven't any resemblance to ours!

An old maid in the land of Aloha
Got wrapped in the coils of a boa;
    And as the snake squeezed,
    The old maid, not displeased,
Cried: "Oh, darling! I love it! Samoa!"

A fellow who fucked but as few can
Had a fancy to try with a toucan;
   He admits, like a man,
   The collapse of his plan:
"I can't – but I bet none of you can!"

     A slow-footed stockman called Beales,
     Slipped up with a bull at his heels;
        Whilst trying to rise,
        He got quite a surprise,
     Learning something of how a cow feels.

     CYRIL MOUNTJOY

There was a young man from New York,
Whose morals were lighter than cork;
   "Bald eagles," said he,
   "Hold no terrors for me:
No, the bird I most fear is the stork!"

     To his bride said a novice named Terence:
     "I do hope you will show some forebearance;
        My sexual habits
        I've picked up from rabbits,
     And, occasionally, watching my parents!"

A round-bottomed gal from Mobile,
Longed for years to be screwed by a seal;
   But down at the Zoo,
   They declared: "No can do!"
Though the seal was hot for the deal.

I'm glad pigs can't fly said young Sellers
(He's one of those worrying fellers);
   "For, if they could fly,
   They'd shit in the sky,
And we'd all have to carry umbrellas!"

RON RUBIN

     Two she-camels spied on a goat:
     One jealously said: "You will note
       She leaves the Sheik's tent
       With her tail oddly bent,
     And great clumps of hair pulled from her coat!"

As dull as the life of the cloister
(Except it's a little bit moister),
  Mutatis mutandum
  Non est disputandum –
There's no thrill in sex for the oyster.

     Kept "late at the office" the charmer,
     Coming home to a warm bath felt calmer;
       "So easy," he thought,
       "The wife suspects naught."
     But the bathtub was filled with piranha!

A platinum blonde, Goldilocks,
Who kept a *ménage* near the docks,
   Had it off with three bears
   Near Wapping Old Stairs,
And infected them all with the pox.

FIONA PITT-KETHLEY

        An aristocratic old Count,
        Who fell madly in love with his mount,
           Said: "My status enables
           Behaviour in stables
        For which I'm not *bound* to account!"

A bestial artist named Victor,
Had acquired a boa constrictor;
   He'd intended to sketch her,
   But decided (the lecher!)
To fuck instead of depicting her.

        An Italian rider named Toni,
        Consumes far too much steamed macaroni;
           She doesn't mind that
           She's becoming so fat -
        She'll just bounce if she falls off her pony.

There was a young lady from Teal,
Who was raped in the lake by an eel;
   One morning at dawn,
   She gave birth to a prawn,
Two small fish, and a whiskery seal!

There was a young man of St Paul,
Whose prick was exceedingly small;
  He could bugger a bug
  That he'd found in a rug,
And the bug hardly felt it at all.

The notorious Duchess of Peels,
Watched a fisherman fishing for eels;
  Said she: "Would you mind?
  Shove one up my behind –
I am curious to know how it feels."

Thus spake an old Chinese mandarin:
"There's a subject I'll choose to use candour in:
    The geese of Peking
    Are so familiar with sin,
They'd as soon let a man as a gander in."

        A fox-hound retired from the hunt,
        When he found that his lobes had grown blunt
            To the scent of a fox,
            But he still sniffed the rocks
        For the mystical fragrance of cunt.

A red-arsed and randy baboon,
That resides by the River Rangoon;
    Fucks each one of the women
    That come to go swimming,
By the light of the silvery moon.

        There once was a clergyman's daughter,
        Who detested the pony he'd bought her;
            Till she found that its dong
            Was as hard and as long
        As the prayers that her father had taught her.

One morning old Mahatma Gandhi,
Had a hard-on, and it was so dandy;
    He called to an aide:
    "Please, quick, bring me a maid,
Or a nanny goat, whichever's handy."

Her tubby young hubby, named Tony,
Discovered her fucking a pony;
   Said he: "What's it got
   My dear, that I've not?"
Sighed she: "Just a yard-long poloni!"

      There was a young man from Australia,
      Who went on a wild bacchanalia;
         He buggered five frogs,
         Several mice and some dogs,
      And a bishop in fullest regalia!

A well-endowed chap, a Maltese,
Who could even screw horses with ease,
   Bypassed natural laws
   In this manner because
Of his dong, which hung down to his knees.

      It is the unfortunate habit,
      Of the rabbit to breed like a rabbit;
         One can state, without question,
         This must lead to congestion
      In the burrows that rabbits inhabit.

There was a young lady of Wohl's Hill,
Who sat herself down on a mole's hill;
   The resident mole
   Stuck his head up her hole –
Now, the lady's all right, but the mole's ill.

An exhausted old chap from Bangor,
Said to his insatiable whore:
   "If you'd like to roll over,
   I'll fetch my dog Rover,
And you can have eight inches more!"

        A tight-fisted farmer of Neep,
        Was so keen to live life on the cheap,
           When he wanted to screw,
           There was nothing to do
        But act out his desires with sheep.

A farmhand from outside Adair,
Decided he'd diddle a mare;
   He leapt up a ladder
   And jolly well had her,
Dungarees down and arse in the air.

        A broken-down harlot named Tupps,
        Was heard to confess in her cups:
           "The height of my folly
           Was fucking that collie –
        But I'll get a good price for the pups."

A fisherman near Cape Cod,
Said: "I'll bugger that tuna, by God!"
   But the high-minded fish
   Resented his wish,
And swam swiftly off with his rod!

Though we study the birds and the bees,
Why on earth choose examples like these?
   There's no clear connection
   Between bees and erection,
And most birds do it up in the trees!

        An elderly farmer near Nice,
        Who was long past desire for a piece,
           Would jack off his hogs,
           And his cows and his dogs,
        Till his parrot alerted the police.

Poor farmers obsessed with the itch,
Have, because they are never that rich,
   To harbour their tails
   In all kinds of females –
Be they Rhode Island Red, sow or bitch.

        A keeper of bees came to grief,
        With a sting that was awkward, though brief;
           He got over the shock
           When he found that his cock
        Was a plonker that beggared belief!

        JOHN SLIM

When asked by the Duchess at tea,
If an eggplant I ever did see,
   I said: "Yes," rather bored;
   Replied she: "You've explored
Up a hen's ass much further than me!"

An old spinster in Kalamazoo,
Once strolled after dark through the zoo;
   She was seized by the nape
   Of her neck by an ape,
And remembers: "My God! What a screw!"

But how he never phones, never writes...

There was a young Nubian prince,
Whose cock would make elephants wince;
   While socking the sperm
   To a large pachyderm,
He slipped, and he's not been seen since.

There was an old man from near here,
Who got awfully drunk on strong beer;
   He fell in a ditch,
   And some son-of-a-bitch
Of a bulldog fucked him in his ear.

       There was a young man of Bengal,
       Who went to a Fancy Dress Ball;
          His ridiculous stunt
          To dress up as a cunt,
       Got him fucked by a dog in the hall.

A habit obscene and bizarre,
Has taken ahold of Papa;
   He brings home young camels,
   And other odd mammals,
And gives them a go at Mama.

       There was a young man of Seattle,
       Who bested a bull in a battle;
          With fire and gumption,
          He assumed the bull's function,
       And deflowered a whole herd of cattle.

There once was a man of Belfast,
Whose balls out of iron were cast;
   He'd managed somehow
   To bugger a sow,
Thus you get pig-iron, at last.

One evening a workman named Rawls,
Fell asleep in his old overalls;
    But when he woke up he
    Discovered his puppy
Had bitten off both of his balls.

On the plains of north-central Tibet,
They have thought of the strangest thing yet:
    On the ass of a camel,
    They pour blue enamel,
And bugger the beast while it's wet.

A big hairy dog named McFee,
Has a lot of old friends he must see;
    So he wanders the streets
    On all four of his feet,
But he visits them largely on three.

        A terrified lady named Brewster,
        Had a dream that a rooster seduced her;
            She awoke with a scream,
            It was only a dream –
        And a lump in the mattress had goosed her.

Amelia was one of those dames,
Who excelled at the jolliest games,
    She was such fun to lay:
    Her pudenda would play
Obligatos, and call you cute names!

        There was a young nudist, quite bare,
        Who had an affair with a bear;
            But the surly old brute,
            With a snap of her snoot,
        Left him one measly ball and some hair.

A pernickety maiden named Florence,
Had declared she found sex an abhorrence;
    Till they found her in bed,
    With her pussy all red,
And her Rottweiler spending in torrents!

There was a young girl of Eau Claire,
Who, when chased by a ravenous bear,
   Ran over a field,
   But tripped and revealed
Some meat to the bear that was rare.

     A keeper in Regent's Park Zoo,
     Tried to fuck a female kangaroo;
       But she zipped up her pouch,
       And the rascal cried: "Ouch!
     You've got half of my whanger in you!"

An old country maid from Nantucket,
Had an asshole as big as a bucket;
   While bent over the oven,
   A-dreamin' of lovin',
Her goat seized the moment to fuck it!

     A shepherd from Gwent's rolling hills,
     Was persistently searching for thrills,
       Till a sheep he molested,
       Quite rightly protested,
     And sent him the veterinary bills.

Your name, little dog, is so apt;
You are sweet, but you ought to be slapped.
   You're known as a Shih-Tzu,
   Which certainly fits you,
Considering how you've just crapped!

JOHN SLIM

A disgusting young chap named MacGill,
Made his neighbours exceedingly ill,
When they learned of his habits
Involving tame rabbits,
And a bird with a flexible bill.

There once was a dear little deer,
Who was licking her dear little rear;
She explained: "With some luck,
I shall spot a big buck –
And, with more luck, the buck will stop here!"

JOHN SLIM

Most uncommonly fond of her snake,
An exotic young maiden thus spake:
   "If my good friend, the boa
   Shoots his spermatozoa,
Oh, what offspring we'll leave in our wake!"

     In a meadow a chap named Llewellyn,
     Had a dream he was buggering Helen;
       When he woke he discovered
       A prize bull had him covered,
     With bollocks as big as a melon!

All the lady-apes fled from King Kong –
Whose great dong was unspeakably long;
   Though a passing giraffe
   Quaffed his yard-and-a-half,
And ecstatically burst into song!

     Enrique, a lonely young squirrel,
     Lived at home with his Mum in the Wirral;
       He'd had quite a yen
       For an overweight hen,
     Till she told him her real name was Cyril!

     IAN HERBERT

There was a young girl called Priscilla,
Who flavoured her cunt with vanilla;
    The taste was so fine,
    Men and beasts stood in line,
Though she called it a day at Godzilla!

                I will freely admit I love fellas,
                And gorillas and monkeys, as well as
                    Young apes and baboons,
                    And the handles of brooms –
                Such a whore! (like I once had a spell as).

There once was a girl named Miss Randall,
Who kept a young bear cub to dandle;
    Said she: "At a pinch,
    This grizzlie's six-inch
Is a fine substitute for a candle."

                A frustrated farmer named Raines,
                With a head full of bollocks for brains,
                    Climbed up on a stool
                    To consort with a mule,
                And got kicked in the prick for his pains.

There once was a maid from Geneva,
Who kept a giraffe to relieve her;
    The result of such fucking
    Was a four-legged duckling,
Several eggs, and a spotted retriever!

A bat and a bat in a cave,
Were wondering which one was Dave;
   It's hard in the dark
   To tell them apart,
But the bat with the balls must be fave.

      There is a young fellow named Price,
      Who dabbles in all kinds of vice:
         He has virgins, and boys,
         And mechanical toys,
      And, on Tuesdays, he meddles with mice!

An Olympian lecher called Zeus,
Found a lady called Leda to goose;
   You might say it's not on,
   Being goosed by a swan –
But with Zeus on the loose, what's the use?

JOHN SLIM

      A student who hailed from St John's,
      Badly wanted to bugger the swans;
         "Goodness, no!" said a porter,
         "Please, bugger my daughter –
      Them swans is reserved for the dons!"

"They A' Do't"

The grit folk an' the puir do't,
The blyte folk an' the sour do't,
    The black, the white,
    Rude an'polite,
Baith autocrat an' boor do't.

For they a' do't – they a' do't,
The beggars an' the braw do't,
    Folk that ance were,
    An' folk that are –
The folk that come will a' do't.

    The auld folk try't,
    The young ane's spy't,
An' straightway kiss an' fa' to't,
    The blind, the lame,
    The wild, the tame,
In warm climes an' in cauld do't.

The licensed by the law to't,
Forbidden folk an' a' do't,
    An' priest an' nun
    Enjoy the fun,
An' never ance say na' to't.

The goulocks an' the snails do't,
The cushie-doos an' quails do't,
    The dogs, the cats,
    The mice, the rats,
E'en elephants an' whales do't.

The weebit cocks an' hens do't,
The ribins an' the wrens do't,
 The grizzy bears,
 The toads an' hares,
The paddocks in the fens do't.

The boars an' kangaroos do't,
The titlins an' cuckoos do't,
 While sparrows sma'
 An' rabbits a'
In countless swarms an' crews do't.

The midges, fleas an' bees do't,
The mawkes an' mites in cheese do't,
 An' cault earthworms
 Crawl up in swarms,
An'underneath the trees do't.

The kings an' queens an' a' do't,
The sultan an' pacha do't,
 An' Spanish dons
 Loup off their thrones,
Pu' doon their breeks, an fa' to't.

For they a' do't – they a' do't,
The grit as weel's the sma' do't
 Frae crowned king
 To creeping thing,
'Tis just the same – they a' do't!

Instead of the usual flunkies,
Her Ladyship's tried sex with monkeys,
    Whose appendages vary
    From big and quite scary
To small but acceptably chunky.

      "I'm in luck, I'm in luck, I'm in luck!"
      Thought a man of a Muscovy Duck;
        But, as feathers were flying,
        He heard the bird crying –
      "A mistake? You're a drake? Oh, well – fuck!"

There once was a young man named Cyril
Who was had in a wood by a squirrel;
    And he liked it so good
    That he stayed in the wood
Just as long as the squirrel stayed virile.

The sheep all adore Farmer Giles,
He is always so friendly, all smiles;
    But, once he's got their trust,
    He indulges his lust
Up against walls or bent over stiles.

      If for all sorts of seabirds you yearn,
      There are several statistics you'll learn:
        It's true there is nothing
        Like stuffing a puffin,
      And it's well worth the wait for your tern!

"I'm dreadfully sorry," Fred cried,
"My car hit your rooster. It's died!
    I'd like to replace it."
    "Well, if you can face it,"
Said the farmer, "The hens are outside."

A fastidious schoolman, named Grigg,
Remarked as he buggered his pig:
    "One can't save one's sperm
    Till the end of the term,
And frigging is so infra dig."

CORNELIUS DOYLE

A vigilant watchdog called Mary*,
Would hector us all to be wary
    Of pimps and pornographers,
    Naughty photographers,
And anything nasty and hairy.

RON RUBIN
*Mary Whitehouse.

The vicar of Dunstan St Just,
All consumed with a bestial lust,
    Raped the Bishop's prize fowls,
    Fucked a few startled owls,
And buggered a buzzard that bust!

There was a young lady called Sue,
Who had an affair with a gnu;
    But her sister Priscilla,
    Preferred a gorilla –
Said Sue: "Well, chacun a son gout!"

RON RUBIN

A lusty young lady, named Gwen,
Who had tired of the failures of men,
    Found a horse of red blood
    Which was fresh from the stud,
And only said "Nay!" now and then!

A gorilla that lives in the zoo,
Gets so bored with so little to do,
   He waves his long dong
   And hoses the throng –
Watch out! Next time it might be you.

    Said a tiger, with withering glance,
    To a mouse he'd encountered by chance:
       "Between these four walls,
       Why do mice have small balls?"
    And the mouse said: "Not many can dance!"

    JOHN SLIM

A Southern hillbilly named Hollis,
Used possums and snakes as his solace;
   His offspring had scales,
   And prehensile tails,
And all voted for Governor Wallace.

    One Christmas a spinster named Thrasher,
    After three drinks grew bolder and brasher;
       First she screwed Santa Claus,
       Then, with barely a pause,
    Donner, Blitzen, and, finally, Dasher!

A stately giraffe, when he necks,
Or a hippo when he's having sex,
    Aren't worth a tut-tut
    To the bellowing rut
Of the great Tyrannosaurus Rex.

When raped by four apes in Rangoon,
Said a torrid young tourist named June:
    "I adored the wild screwing
    Those gorillas were doing,
But why did they all come so soon?"

At the table sat young Lord Colquhoun,
With his pet, an old red-arsed baboon;
    His mother said: "Cholmondley,
    I do not think it comely
To encourage that creature to moon!"

Did you know that the Duchess of Riva,
Goes to bed with her golden retriever?
    Says the disgusted Duke:
    "Such a thing makes me puke –
Were it not for her money, I'd leave her!"

There was an old Greek God called Zeus,
And maidens he loved to seduce;
    Disguised as a swan,
    Or a bull – or anon –
He would screw them, then quickly vamoose.

RON RUBIN

An insatiable farmer named Blades,
Has a penchant for busty milk-maids,
    But both donkeys and whores,
    And the knotholes in doors
Are by no means exempt from his raids!

Grown-up words seem to score quite a hit
With Tommy, aged three-and-a-bit;
   Dog and not doggie,
   But pussy not moggie,
And then he found Winnie the Shit!

JOHN SLIM

She has marks on her knees which she shows,
And agrees a grazed knee is what goes
   With love doggy-style –
   But explains, with a smile,
There's no other way the dog knows!

The harlots of London are frightful,
And the fairies, my dear – they're so spiteful!
   I'm no longer on heat,
   For I've happened to meet
A young sheep in Hyde Park – quite delightful!

There was a strange fellow from Dover
Who yearned for a romp in the clover;
   But he gave not one damn
   For woman or man –
The clue was his cry of: "Here, Rover!"

Another young chap from Nantucket,
Took a pig to a thicket to fuck it;
   Said the pig: "No, I'm queer –
   Get away from my rear,
Come around to the front and I'll suck it!"

There was a young man from Geneva,
Who buggered a black bitch retriever;
   The result was a sow,
   Two piglets, a cow,
Several horses, a duck, and a beaver!

There was a young girl of Batonger,
Used to diddle herself with a conger;
   When asked how it feels
   To be pleasured by eels,
She replied: "Like a man, only longer!"

6.
The Devil Named Dick, his Prick, and Other Cocks, Rods, and Todgers

A fellow with passions quite gingery,
Was exploring his young sister's lingerie;
   Then, with giggles of pleasure,
   He plundered her treasure –
Adding incest to insult and injury.

      With a maiden a chap once begat,
      Bouncing triplets named Pat, Nat and Tat;
         'Twas fun in the breeding,
         But hell in the feeding –
      There wasn't a spare tit for tat!

King Henry the Eighth was a Tudor,
Of our monarchs we know of few lewder;
   Each wench that he wed,
   He led straight to bed
Where he viewed'er and wooed'er and screwd'er!

      There was a young fellow, of Lyme,
      Who lived with three wives at a time;
         When asked; "Why the third?"
         He said: "One is absurd,
      And bigamy, sir, is a crime!"

There is an old chap, from St Paul's,
Who reads Harper's Bazaar and McCall's;
   He's developed such passion
   For feminine fashion,
He's knitted a snood for his balls!

To his wife said Sir Humphrey le Dawes:
"Fix this chastity belt to your drawers!"
   But an amorous Celt
   Found the key to the belt,
While the Squire was away at the wars.

A saucy greengrocer in Leeds,
Satisfies women customers' needs:
   'Twixt his apples and pears
   He displays his proud wares –
His satsumas are frequently squeezed!

ANNE RUSSON

Said a certain old Earl that I knew:
"I've been struck from the rolls of Who's Who,
   Just because I was found
   Rolling round on the ground
With a housemaid – and very nice too!"

Said a chap of his small Morris Minor:
"For petting, it couldn't be finer;
   But for love's consummation,
   A wagon called 'station'
Would offer a playground diviner!"

A bloke, in a bus queue in Stoke,
Unzippered his flies for a joke:
   One old chap gave a shout
   And almost passed out,
While a lady nearby had a stroke.

An experienced hooker, Arlene,
Insists: "Give me a lad of eighteen –
   His pecker's much harder,
   There's more cream in his larder,
And he fucks with a vigour obscene!"

There was a young man, Mr Hubber-Dub,
Who belonged to the Suck, Fuck & Bugger Club;
   The great joy of his life
   Were the tits of his wife –
One real, the other India-Rubber, bub!

      Said an urgent young sailor called Mickey,
      As his girl eyed his stiff, throbbing dickey:
         "Pet, my leave's almost up,
         And I need a good tup –
      So bend down and I'll slip you a quickie!"

There was a young stud from Missouri,
Who fucked with astonishing fury,
   Till taken to court
   For his vigorous sport,
And condemned by a poorly hung jury.

      There was a young man, from Racine,
      Who invented a fucking machine;
         Concave or convex
         It would suit either sex,
      With attachments for those in between.

A practical chappie named Wyatt,
Kept a sizeable girl on the quiet;
    And, down by the wharf,
    There was also a dwarf –
In case he should go on a diet.

    There was a young fellow named Willy,
    Who acted remarkably silly;
        At an All-Nations Ball,
        Dressed in nothing at all,
    He claimed that his costume was Chile!

    A precocious young rascal, named Tarr,
    Had a habit of goosing his Ma;
        "Go and pester your sister,"
        She said, when he kissed her,
    "I have trouble enough with your Pa!"

There's this to be said for Verdicchio**,
That whenever the going gets sticchio,
    It increases the strength
    And the breadth and the length
When applied to the gentleman's pricchio...

CYRIL RAY
** *Verdicchio – a dry, white wine from eastern Italy*

There was a young lady of Exeter,
So pretty that men craned their necks at her;
   And one was so brave
   As to take out and wave
The distinguishing sign of his sex at her!

       An insatiable fellow named Dice,
       Noted: "Though they say bigamy's nice;
          Even two are a bore,
          I'd prefer three, or more –
       For the plural of spouse, it *is* spice!"

A well-endowed chap from Coblenz,
Whose appendage was simply immense,
   Employed several draymen,
   A priest and three laymen
To carry it thither and thence!

       A bashful young chap, christened Cleary,
       Was becoming reclusive, well – nearly,
          Till a lassie named Lou
          Showed him how and with who
       He could render his evenings more cheery.

The good vessel's name was Venus,
Its mast was a towering penis;
   Her figurehead
   Was a harlot in bed –
A wonderful sight, aye, by Jesus!

You'll never know how good you are,
Till you try to make love in a car;
    Many men meet defeat
    On a darkened back seat,
And it's only the experts break par.

    A workman who dwelt in Wyre Piddle,
    Met a maiden and posed her a riddle:
        "I find I'm afire
        With carnal desire –
    My poker is hot, is your griddle?"

A lithesome male dancer from Ipswich,
Took the most unbelievable skips, which
   So delighted a miss,
   She demanded a kiss –
He responded: "A kiss on which lips, miss?"

     At the orgy I humped twenty-two,
     And was glad when the whole thing was through;
        I don't find it swinging
        To do all this change-ringing,
     But, at orgies, what else can you do?

A well-endowed nudist, from Ongar,
Sports a cock that's considerably longer,
   Than the average man;
   When he tops up his tan,
It loks like he's captured a conger.

GEOFF HARRIS

     FOR WIDOWER – wanted, housekeeper,
     Not too bloody refined, a light sleeper;
        When employer's inclined
        Must be game for a grind,
     Pay: generous, mind, but can't keep her.

There was an old bounder of Fife,
Who lived a lascivious life;
   When his organ was limp,
   Like an over-boned shrimp,
He brought what was left to his wife.

Come and see our French goods – you can try 'em.
Ensure they're the right size when you buy 'em:
   Strong, smooth, and reversible,
   The thinnest dispersible;
Any odd shape you need, we supply 'em!

     On a date with a charming young bird,
     His erotical feelings were stirred;
       So with bold, virile pluck,
       He enquired: "Do you fuck?"
     She said: "Yes. But, please, don't use that word!"

A rapscallion, far gone in treachery,
Lured maids to their doom with his lechery:
   He invited them in
   For the purpose of sin,
Though he said 'twas to look at his etchery!

     The enjoyment of sex, although great,
     Is in later years said to abate;
       This may well be so,
       But how would I know?
     I'm only a hundred-and-eight!

The orgy began on the lawn,
Several hours ahead of the dawn;
   We found ourselves viewing
   Forty-four couples screwing,
But by sun up they'd all come, and gone.

There was an old chap on a bus,
Who got tangled up in his truss;
   Though the problem was tiny,
   Two grannies cried: "Blimey!
It looks like a big one to us!"

      There was an old Welshman, called Morgan,
      Who had a magnificent organ;
         Said his wife: "You are blessed
         With the absolute best
      Hammond Organ in all of Glamorgan!"

"On the beach," said John sadly, "there's such
A thing as revealing too much."
   So he closed both his eyes
   At the ranks of bare thighs,
And felt his way through them by touch.

ISAAC ASIMOV

      There was an old monarch, called Harry,
      Whose efforts were doomed to miscarry;
         His desire for a son,
         Plus unlimited fun,
      Made him marry and marry and marry.

A sailor, ashore in Peru,
Said: "Signora, quanto por la screw?"
   "For only one peso,
   I will, if you say so,
Be buggered, and nibble it too!"

Although Peeping Tom knew it was wrong,
As Godiva (unclothed) rode along,
    He first ogled her bust
    But then, to his disgust,
Realized she was wearing a thong.

There was a young fellow, called Crouch,
Who was courting a girl on a couch;
    She said: "Why not a sofa?"
    And he exclaimed: "Oh, for
Christ's sake shut your mouth while I – ouch!"

VICTOR GRAY

An unfortunate lady named White,
Found herself in a terrible plight:
   A mucker named Tucker
   Had struck her, the fucker,
The bugger, the bastard, the shite!

      A fellow, whose surname is Hunt,
      Trained his prick to perform a slick stunt;
         This versatile spout
         Could be turned inside-out,
      Like a glove, and be used as a cunt!

There was a young fellow named Kimble,
Whose prick was exceedingly nimble;
   But so fragile, so slender,
   And dainty and tender,
He kept it encased in a thimble!

      Prince Charming was worried to bits:
      All the girls in the town had nice tits,
         But no nether part
         Ever captured his heart,
      Till he cried out: "Oh, Cinders, it fits!"

Nostalgic, in old Aberystwyth,
I sat down and made out a list, with
   The names of the rude
   Lovely ladies I'd screwed,
And the chaps I'd gone out and got pissed with.

RON RUBIN

At an orgy old Julius Caesar,
Met a virgin and tried hard to please her;
   Said she: "My name's Mimi,
   Are you pleased to see me,
Or is that the Tower of Pisa?"

        I may look fairly old and sedate,
        But I still enjoy sex, I can't wait;
           I'm still getting my kicks
           At seventy-six,
        Though I'm living at seventy-eight!

A diminutive person, called Willie,
Ran amok through the streets willy-nilly;
   Though they called him "Pervert!",
   In his skimpy nightshirt,
He was never a flasher, just silly!

JANET SMITH

        There was a young chap from Nantucket.
        Whose cock was so long he could suck it;
           He said, with a grin,
           As he wiped off his chin:
        "If my ear was a cunt, I would fuck it!"

We knows three young beauties from Cuxham,
And, whenever we meets 'em, we fucks 'em;
   When that game grows stale,
   We sits on a rail,
And pulls out our cocks, and they sucks 'em!

Whilst cruising the cosmos, McCavity,
Used language of frightful depravity;
   When asked to desist,
   He replied: "I insist –
Out here there is no need for gravity."

RON RUBIN

A certain young fellow, from Buckingham,
Once stood on the old bridge at Ruckingham,
   Perusing the stunts
   Of the cunts in the punts,
And the tricks of the pricks that were fucking 'em!

That push-it-in-double chap (Kent),
Who thought he was coming, but went,
   Now clamps balls to tip
   With a jubilee clip,
Which helps, to a certain extent.

There was an old fellow from Dallas
Who enjoyed doing things with his phallus;
   Such tricks did he try,
   It became, by and by,
Little more than a leather-tough callus.

A satisfied lady called Bridget
Whose man was a masterful midget,
   Said: "I've never yet failed
   To be thrilled when impaled
On his totally out-of-scale widget!"

"At last I've seduced the au pair,
With some steak and a chocolate éclair,
  Some peas and some chips,
  Three Miracle Whips,
And a carafe of vin ordinaire!"

CYRIL RAY

Said a frantic young fellow called Izzy,
Who got the girls into a tizzy,
  By coming so quick
  When they played with his dick:
"I can't wait – I am ever so busy!"

JOHN SLIM

Said Old Father William: "I'm humble,
And getting too old for a tumble;
  But produce me a blonde,
  And I'm still not beyond
An attempt at an interesting fumble!"

CONRAD AIKEN

There was a young outlaw named Hood,
Who lived in a Nottingham wood;
  He learned how to fuck
  From old Friar Tuck,
And made Marian whenever he could.

EO PARROTT

There was a braw Scott from Loch Ness,
Who bragged of his twelve-inch prowess;
   Till the beast of the loch
   Bit off most of his cock,
Now he brags of considerable less.

    There was a young lad, named Jack Horner,
    Who played with his plums in a corner;
       Said his father: "That's sad,
       When I was a lad,
    I preferred a massage down the sauna!"

    FIONA PITT-KETHLEY

An old man at the Folies Bergères,
Had a cock, a most wondrous affair:
   It snipped off a small curl
   From each new chorus girl,
And he's had a wig made from the hair.

    A randy Red Indian Chief,
    Is always in need of relief:
       The scope of the totem
       That goes with his scrotum
    Is something that beggars belief.

    JOHN SLIM

There was a young monarch called Ed,
Who took Mrs Simpson to bed;
    As they bounced up and down,
    He said: "Bugger the crown –
We'll give it to Georgie instead!"

Said a lecherous fellow named Shea,
When his prick would not rise for a lay:
    "You must seize it, and squeeze it,
    And tease it, and please it."
Adding: "Rome wasn't built in a day!"

Of his face she thought not very much,
Only then, at his very first touch,
  Her attitude shifted,
  He was terribly gifted
At frigging and fucking and such.

A young lass got married in Chester,
Her mother both kissed her and blessed her;
  Said she: "You're in luck,
  He's a hell of a fuck –
I've had him myself up in Leicester!"

There was an old chap with a prick,
Which into his wife he would stick;
  Every morning and night,
  If it stood up all right –
Not a very remarkable trick.

A trucker, by name of McWired,
Had a regular whore that he hired
  To fuck when not trucking;
  But trucking plus fucking
Got him so fucking tired he got fired.

A man with a very long dink,
Vaulted home on it, quick as a wink;
  His means of propulsion
  Did not cause revulsion –
He'd passed you before you could blink.

JOHN SLIM

An astonished ex-virgin named Howard,
Remarked, after being deflowered:
 "I knew that connection
 Was made in that section,
But not that it's so darned high-powered!"

Two gardeners, Plantem and Pickem,
Surprised a good lady in Wickam:
 They replied, with a shout,
 To her cry of "Prick out",
"They're out! Tell us where we can stick 'em!"

An unsavoury baker from Tring,
Such a weirdo in matters of sin;
 Often crammed the small crease
 Twixt the legs of his niece
With a foot of his old rolling pin.

An ailing and rich old roué,
Who felt himself slipping away;
 Endowed a large ward
 In a house where he'd whored –
A big crowd at his funeral? I'll say!

I'd rather have fingers than toes.
I'd rather have ears than a nose.
 And, a happy erection
 Brought just to perfection
Makes me terribly sad when it goes.

There was an old fellow of Harrow,
Whose cock was the size of a marrow;
   And as for his balls,
   One neighbour recalls
That he wheeled them about in a barrow!

RON RUBIN

A well-endowed gent near Ghent,
His entire monthly income all spent,
   Shows his organs, at large,
   For a small handling charge
To assist him in paying his rent.

Said Jack: "Do you think we should sort of
Seek the spice that our love life is short of?"
   Said Jill: "Good idea!
   From things that I hear,
Foreplay is quite highly thought of!"

There was a young fellow named Bowen,
Whose pecker kept growen and growen;
   It grew so tremendous,
   So gross and horrendous,
It was no good for fucking – just showen.

Said the potentate gross and despotic:
"My tastes are more rich than exotic;
   I have always adored
   Making love in a Ford –
I suppose I am auto-erotic."

There was a young man of Cape Cod,
Who put others' wives into pod;
   His surname was Tucker,
   The dirty old fucker,
The bugger, the blighter, the sod!

A licentious old justice of Salem,
Used to catch all the harlots and jail 'em;
   But instead of a fine,
   He would stand them in line,
Take his common-law tool and impale 'em.

There is a young man in Hong Kong,
With a wondrous trifurcated prong:
 A small one for sucking,
 A larger for fucking,
And a belter for beating a gong!

   The favourite pastime of grandfather,
   Is tickling his balls with a feather;
    But the thing he likes best,
    Out of all of the rest,
   Is knocking them gently together.

A glutted debauchee from Frome,
Lured beauteous maids to his room;
 Where after he'd strip 'em,
 He'd generally whip 'em
With bundles of twigs or a broom.

   The life of a clerk of the session,
   Was strangled in psychic repression,
    But his maladies ceased
    When his penis uncreased
   In straight geometric progression.

As he creamed my wife's cunt, the stud said:
"I could fuck this until I was dead!"
 As he plugged up her trough,
 I jerked myself off:
"If that's how you feel, go ahead!"

"Hello! You're a nympho they claim,"
Said Fred, "You're a good-looking dame.
   They tell me you choose
   Only cowboys or Jews –
Hopalong Goldberg's the name…"

JOHN SLIM

In a haunted old house on the coast,
With his willy as stiff as a post,
   Was a bare-bottomed lad
   Doing press-ups like mad –
He explained he was laying a ghost!

JOHN SLIM

A well-endowed bounder named Blood,
Made a fortune performing at stud,
   With a fifteen-inch peter,
   A double-beat metre,
And a load like a biblical flood.

        When his prick wouldn't rise for a lay,
        Said a languorous bounder named Shea,
           "You must seize it, and squeeze it
           And otherwise please it,
        But, dear, Rome wasn't built in a day!"

There was a young fellow named Chisholm,
So afflicted by skin erotism,
   Whilst bathing, he'd rub
   His prick in the tub,
Till the water was soapy with jism.

        There was a young person from Brum,
        With a todger much longer than some;
           "My banjo" he called it,
           The girls were enthralled, it
        Was always a pleasure to strum.

        JOHN SLIM

There was a young man from Winsocket,
Who put a girl's hand in his pocket;
   Her delicate touch
   Thrilled his pecker so much,
It shot off in the air like a rocket.

A sailor who'd slept in the sun,
Woke to find his fly-buttons undone;
   He observed, with a smile:
   "Goodness me! A sundial!
And, my word – it's a quarter past one!"

      An ingenious fellow named Meek,
      Has devised a new lingual technique;
         It drives women frantic,
         But, far less romantic,
      It's wearing the hair from his cheek.

An old exhibitionist, Pete,
Who is nothing if not indiscreet,
   Fondled his dong
   Till it grew very long,
And actually dragged in the street.

      A eunuch, I've oft heard it said,
      Was a wonderful lover in bed;
         It appears no sultana
         Could detect, from his manner,
      That he'd used a banana instead!

A dismissive young chap from Belgravia,
Who cared neither for God nor his Saviour;
   Promenaded the Strand
   With his cock in his hand,
And was jailed for indecent behaviour.

A lazy old bounder, named Betts,
Is as idle as anyone gets
 Till along comes a gal,
 Offers: "I'll fuck you, pal."
And if she'll do the work, he says: "Let's!"

All those small cocks (on which we won't dwell)
Looked no bigger encouraged to swell;
 I've endured the tedium
 Of others, classed medium,
But, at last – I've discovered XL!

There was a young man named Ignatius,
Who lived in a garret (quite spacious);
 When he visited Aunty's,
 He always wore panties,
But, alone in his garret – good gracious!

A self-contained fellow named Beams,
Has such little regard for wet dreams,
 That, if lacking a whore,
 He will bore out the core
Of an apple, or fuck fondant creams.

A randy old dandy named Dick,
Liked to feel young girls' hands on his prick;
 He taught them to fool
 With his weather-worn tool
Till the cream shot out, lovely and thick.

The prick of a young man at Kew,
Displayed veins that were azure of hue;
   Its head was quite red,
   So he waved it and said:
"Three cheers for the red, white and blue!"

There was a young fellow too smart,
To be trapped by affairs of the heart;
   When safely in bed,
   He cautiously said:
"I am yours until dawn us do part."

JOHN SLIM

As a trainee upholsterer, he
Was taught woodwork and embroidery;
   And though bottom caning
   Required some explaining,
He applied birch and rattan with glee.

JANET SMITH

      The King gave a lesson in class,
      Whilst instructing a naive young lass;
         When she used the word "Damn",
         He rebuked her: "Please, ma'am –
      Keep a more civil tongue in my ass!"

An erudite fellow of Buckingham,
Wrote a treatise on pussies and sucking 'em;
   But later, this work
   Was eclipsed by a Turk
Whose subject was assholes and fucking 'em.

      The legendary Prince of Sirocco,
      Had erotical penchants rococo;
         The prick of this prince
         Was flavoured with quince,
      And his semen was seasoned with cocoa.

An arrogant bastard named Ben,
Would elongate his pecker, and then
   Satisfy front and rear,
   Which made him the dear
Of the girls, and the envy of men.

There is a young man of Devizes,
Whose balls are incredible sizes;
   And a tool, when at ease,
   That hangs down to his knees;
Goodness knows what it's like when it rises!

      There was a young lady from Alnwicke,
      A devilish cad caused to panic;
         For he frigged her and fucked her,
         And buggered and sucked her,
      With a glee barely short of satanic.

A young motorcyclist from Horton,
Whose tool's a particularly short 'un,
   Makes up for the loss
   With the balls of a hoss,
And the stroke of a 500 Norton!

      Old Fred never dallied or dithered:
      If he spotted a slot, up he slithered;
         His excitable dick
         Meant he had to be quick,
      Or, before he had slithered – he'd withered.

      JOHN SLIM

There was a young fellow named Keach,
Who fell fast asleep on the beach;
   He dreamt of nude women,
   His proud organ brimming
And squirting on all within reach.

237

I lost my arm in the army,
I lost my leg in the navy.
   I lost my balls
   Over Niagara Falls,
And I lost my cock in a lady.

Though his willy was widely admired,
It wouldn't enlarge when required;
   Then one day it dawned
   That it did when he yawned,
Since then, he's enjoyed being tired.

JOHN SLIM

Said Jock: "As a cock, it's just fine;
As hard as a rock, and it's mine,
   But it glows on erection
   (A torch-like projection)
Which means I get called Rise-and-Shine!"

JOHN SLIM

     Under the spreading chestnut tree,
     The village smithy sat,
        Amusing himself
        Abusing himself,
     And catching his load in his hat.

There was a young man from Vancouver,
Whose existence had lost its prime mover;
   But the loss he supplied
   With a buffalo hide,
Two pears, and the bag from a Hoover.

     That devious pervert McNick,
     Made good use of the shape of his dick:
        He painted the shaft
        Like a lolly, and laughed
     As he offered young ladies a lick.

There was an old fellow named Quart,
Whose prick, although thick, was quite short;
   To make up for his loss
   He had balls like a hoss,
And he never spent less than a quart.

Said a lad with no balls: "None's enough, as
The fillies have found no one suffers;
   It works like a dream:
   They bonk at full steam,
And never collide with the buffers!"

JOHN SLIM

       Oh, the worker is nobody's fool,
       For, by rights, he's the man with the tool;
          His ponderous prick'll
          Arise with the sickle,
       And bugger the buggers who rule.

I chase all the girls when I'm spunky:
I'm a five-days-a-week sexual junkie,
   Though I tend not to stray
   Either Tues or Wednesday –
On those nights I just spank my own monkey.

       Said a President prone to give pecks,
       To those areas other than necks:
          "Although this is sultry,
          It is not adult'ry –
       I'm not even sure if it's sex!"

A well-endowed guy named Apollo,
Remarked as he larked in a hollow:
   "My darling, my dong
   Is twelve inches long."
Said she: "That's a hard one to swallow!"

In Eden, the first man, called Adam,
Went up to his Eve, and said: "Madam,
    I've always been true,
    There's been no one but you –
If there had been, you bet I'd have had 'em!"

RON RUBIN

A fortuitous fellow named Morgan,
Possessed the most unusual organ:
    The end of his dong,
    Fully twelve inches long,
Had a number of heads, like a gorgon!

An insatiable farmer named Grant,
Whose behaviour is simply gallant;
   Has fucked all his dozens
   Of nieces and cousins,
In addition, of course, to his aunt.

     The cock of a charmer named Gable,
     Was as pliant and long as a cable;
       And each night as they ate,
       This confirmed reprobate
     Always screwed his wife under the table.

A piratical chap from Penzance
Jolly-rogered his three maiden aunts;
   Though they'd each been defiled,
   He ne'er got them with child,
Utilizing the letters of France.

     There's a café in old Milton Keynes,
     Where the waiter wears very tight jeans,
       With an awfully large bulge
       Which, when asked, he'll divulge
     Is in fact seven tins of baked beans.

There is a young bounder named Fink,
Who possesses a very tart dink;
   To sweeten it some
   He steeps it in rum,
And it's driving the ladies to drink.

A cautious young fellow named Tunney,
Had a cock that was worth any money;
   When eased in halfway,
   The girl's gasp made him say:
"Why the sigh?" "For the rest of it, honey!"

There is a young bounder from Barrow,
Whose cock-bone is lacking in marrow;
   To accomplish a fuck,
   He uses tape (duct),
And feathers the shaft like an arrow.

A lecherous fellow named Babbit,
Asked a girl if she'd fuck it or nab it;
   Said she: "From long habit,
   I fuck like a rabbit,
So I'd rather cohabit than grab it!"

A well-endowed chap with a cock,
Several sizes too big for his jock,
   Eventually found
   It was far better wound
Round one leg and tucked into his sock!

The sex-mad young son of Lord Bicester,
Made love to his mother and sicester;
   But when he got laid
   With the new parlour maid,
His Pa said "Enough!" and dismicester.

RON RUBIN

There once was a fellow named Danny,
The size of whose prick was uncanny;
   His wife, the poor dear,
   Took it into her ear,
And it came out the hole in her fanny.

     A frugal young fellow named Wise,
     Gets the most from the dead whores he buys;
        After sporting a while,
        As a gay necrophile,
     For dessert he has maggot surprise.

A self-centred bastard named Newcombe,
Who seduced lots of girls but made few come,
   Said: "The pleasures of tail
   Were ordained for the male.
I'm all right. Do I care whether you come?"

     In a hammock a bounder named Bliss,
     Was engaging a cautious young miss;
        She wriggled and squirmed
        So as not to get spermed,
     And they ended up something like this.

Captain Dick's dick refused to go down,
When they laid him to rest in the ground;
   "Here lies," says the stone,
   "A sea-dog with his bone."
In the absence of words more profound.

Two little girlies from Twickenham,
Two naughty boys with their prick in 'em;
   They lay on the sward,
   And prayed to the Lord
To lengthen and strengthen and thicken 'em.

        There was a young fellow named Tucker,
        Who, instructing a novice cock-sucker,
           Said: "Don't bow your lips
           Like an elephant's hips,
        The boys like it best when you pucker."

A well-endowed young able seaman,
Was considered by ladies a demon;
   In peace or in war
   And at sea or on shore,
He could certainly dish out the semen!

        Ladies give Stan's stiff penis a spasm:
        Anytime that he sees 'em or 'as 'em;
           He enjoys them so well,
           He needs only to smell
        Them to have a spontaneous orgasm.

A bit of a wanker named Willy,
Was informed masturbation was silly:
   "You will probably find
   It will make you go blind!"
Still he fondles his cock willy-nilly.

The cock of a fellow named Randall,
Emits sparks like a large roman candle;
   He is much in demand,
   For the colours are grand,
But the girls find him too hot to handle.

       A detective named Ellery Queen,
       Had olfactory powers so keen,
          He could tell, in a flash,
          From the scent of a gash,
       Who its last occupant might have been.

"Look! It's thirty-six inches – a yard!"
Boasted Dick when his prick had grown hard;
   But a bona three-feeter?
   That's never a metre –
It's a con, it's a lie, a charade!

       A handsome young gentleman built
       Like a tank, has no feelings of guilt;
          He sees widows' weeds,
          And he sorts out their needs –
       "Wilt thou?" and they usually wilt.

       JOHN SLIM

A farmer I knew named O'Droole,
Had the most unbelievable tool;
   He would use it to plough,
   Or to diddle a cow,
And sometimes as a cue-stick at pool.

A little old man with a dick,
Twice as long as a sizeable stick,
    Often waves it about,
    Knocking passers-by out –
An annoying but memorable trick.

A meticulous maiden of Streator's
Predilection's to nibble her peters;
    If you ask her, she'll say:
    "I prefer it this way –
And you have to admit, it's much neater!"

I've encountered some cocks in my time:
Each of them celebrated in rhyme;
    One example, from Broome,
    Used to whistle a tune
Not dissimilar to Auld Lang Syne!

        When I was a baby, my penis
        Was as white as the buttocks of Venus;
            But now it's as red
            As her nipples instead –
        All because of the feminine genus!

Mickey's is bigger than Dickie's,
And Dickie's is bigger than Rickie's;
    I like cocks the size
    That bring tears to my eyes,
Although small ones are better for quickies.

        I, Caesar, when I learned of the fame
        Of Cleopatra, I straightway laid claim:
            Ahead of my legions
            I invaded her regions –
        I saw, I conquered, I came!

An innocent maiden from Slough,
Was insistent she didn't know how,
    Till a young bounder caught her,
    And jolly well taught her –
She lodges in Pimlico now!

A contortionist hailing from Lynch,
Used to rent out his tool by the inch;
   A foot cost a quid,
   And he could, so he did,
Stretch it almost to three at a pinch!

        A muscular Scotsman, named Wilt,
        Wore a fashionable mini-kilt;
           When a gentle breeze blew,
           The old ladies gasped: "Phew!
        Yon young lad is extremely well-built."

        DENNIS WALKER

I know of a fortunate Hindu,
Sought after in towns that he's been to
   By the ladies he knows,
   Who are thrilled to their toes
By the tricks he can make his foreskin do.

        No wonder young maidens will cower
        At the thought of bold Owen Glendower:
           They say he has balls
           Like the dome of St Paul's,
        And a prick like the Post Office tower!

In the Garden of Eden lay Adam,
Complacently stroking his madam;
   And loud was his mirth
   For he knew that, on earth,
There were only two balls – and he had 'em!

I do like a nice glass of brandy –
It makes me feel dashing and dandy,
　　And sucks-boo to those
　　Who chose to suppose
I'd be bound to rhyme "brandy" with "randy".

It's not quite the same thing with whisky,
Which is well known for making you frisky,
　　But in Sauchiehall Street,
　　Where they take the stuff neat,
To be frisky on whisky is risky...

CYRIL RAY

An inquisitive chap from Mobile,
Often wondered just how it would feel
　　To carry a gong
　　Hanging down from his dong,
And occasionally let the thing peal.

So he rigged up a clever device,
And tried the thing out once or twice;
　　Though it wasn't the gong
　　But the end of his dong
That peeled, and it didn't feel nice!

My God, he's an impudent fella!
That girl that he showed round the cellar
   Lost her status quo ante
   Between the Chianti
And the magnums of Valpolicella...

Which reminds me of Asti Spumante,
A wine that I'm more pro than anti –
   The only thing is
   That this fizz aphrodis...
iac leads to delicto flagrante!

CYRIL RAY

There was a young fellow named Skinner,
Who took a young lady to dinner;
   At a quarter to nine,
   They sat down to dine,
And, at twenty to ten, it was in her!
  - The dinner, not Skinner –
Skinner was in her before dinner.

There was a young fellow named Tupper,
Who took a young lady to supper;
   At a quarter to nine,
   They sat down to dine,
And, at twenty to ten, it was up her!
   Not the supper, not Tupper –
It was some son-of-a-bitch named Skinner.

I'm the victim of vile sabotage –
I'd set out for the day on the plage
   And a picnic à deux
   With some fruit and Bresse Bleu
(An especially fragrant fromage).

And the prospect of gay persiflage,
But before I could cry: "Soyez sage!"
   The girl I was keen on
   Poured out some young Chinon*
Instead of the old Hermitage** ...

On this tale I need hardly enlarge –
As you so rightly say: "Quelle dommage!"
   For I needed un vin
   That puts strength in a man –
And esprit and élan and courage...

So I went to collect my Delage,
Which I keep in a nearby garage,
   Driving off in a huff
   And proceeding to stuff
The cocotte on the second étage...

CYRIL RAY

* *Chinon – lightish red wine from the Loire.*
** *Hermitage – robust red wine from the Rhône.*

The first time I delved in his smalls,
And caressed well-hung Montague's balls,
   The size was a shock,
   Though, nearby in a sock,
Was the biggest surprise of them all!

      A highwayman, robbing a coach,
      Decided to change his approach –
         Bored stiff simply robbing,
         He'd focus on knobbing
      And just nick the odd wallet or brooch.

Little boys will be boys will be boys:
Hanging up Christmas stockings for toys;
   But when they're fully grown,
   And have minds of their own,
It's the stockings themselves bring the joys!

BETTY PAGE

      An inflatable cock is the thing –
      There is no substitute, once it's in;
         Gaze amazed as it rises,
         It comes in three sizes,
      And does just what it says on the tin!

In the park, where he practised his jogging,
Several couples were actively snogging;
   When such sights met his eyes,
   He gave up exercise
And took up the new hobby of dogging.

A Texan Rhodes Scholar, named Ned,
Was a witty companion in bed;
  With priapic zest
  He would toss off each jest:
"I am standing for Congress," he said.

LYNDON T MOLE

        The Marquis de Sade was a bod,
        Who'd never had much time for God;
          Possessed by the Devil,
          He'd far rather revel
        With some equally like-minded sod!

When she met him, she thought: "Mmm, bit iffy."
And his hairstyle? A trifle too quiffy;
  But the doubts that she held
  Were quite quickly dispelled
When out popped a spectacular stiffy!

        If one cock's not enough for your kicks,
        And you'd sooner have four, five, or six,
          Ensure your next stop's
          At our chain of Sex Shops,
        And select from our new Prick 'n' Mix!

A curious virgin called Ruth,
Had been told her bloke's cock reached the roof,
  And, believing its size
  Might bring tears to her eyes,
Was quite keen for more tangible proof.

Don Juan was an amorous gent,
On sexual pleasure, hell-bent;
    Though bored wives adored him,
    Their husbands abhorred him
And hoped he would prove impotent!

JANET SMITH

When the hour strikes midnight o'clock,
Old Dracula whips out his cock;
    His bite is so quick,
    Just the tiniest prick,
But his dick is a much bigger shock!

I'm in love with a butternut squash.
You may think: What a load of old tosh!
    But its contours are so
    Like a favourite dildo,
I can't help but exclaim: "Golly gosh!"

Young Billy's so fond of his willy,
He will whip it out even when chilly;
    Whilst beating his meat,
    He creates his own heat –
He's not freezing for anyone, silly!

A twelve-inch vermillion cock?
I'm afraid we don't have one in stock;
    Perhaps something else
    That may be on the shelf?
Mind you, I finish work six o'clock!

Even though there's not much of a plot,
Still I whipped out my cock for the shot
    Of a number of floozies
    (Old hands in blue movies)
Gang-wanking me off on the spot!

An unusual fellow named Nick,
Was so terribly proud of his prick,
    With no fear it might bend,
    He would bounce on its end,
Shouting: "Look, it's my own pogo stick!"

Asked a lass, as she strolled down the Strand,
Of her beau, who'd begun to expand:
    "Your cock's catching the eye
    Of each girl passing by –
Can't you cover it up with your hand?"

We enquired about sex around town,
And a BJ was favourite we found;
    So, here's sound advice girls:
    You'll go up in the world,
If you do a good job going down!

A trucker in old Tennessee,
Couldn't see what his future might be;
    With a blow-job in view,
    Would she know what to do?
But she said that she'd suck it and see!

His cock is much bigger than ours,
And we marvel at it in the showers;
  I know this is rude,
  But its length is tattooed
With the names of the girls he deflowers!

Said a discerning lass from Australia:
"Now, concerning the male genitalia –
  Men will brag of their size,
  Till you're sure of a prize
Then exhibit *wee* paraphenalia!"

A pedantic old wanker named Ruin,
Wondered: "Why do we bother with screwing?
    It's safer, and cleaner,
    To fondle your wiener,
And, besides, you can see what you're doing!"

An innocent schoolboy, named Ted,
Fell asleep in a heap on his bed;
        Look! What could be sweeter –
        One hand on his Peter
Pan book, and one under his head?

To her grandson said Grandmother Todd:
"Do you spend the nights rubbing your rod?
    Your Pa, as a kid,
    Most certainly did,
And if you don't, you must be quite odd!"

The dildos have all been marked down,
In the sale at the Sex Shop in town:
        The smallest are free,
        Medium, 30p,
And the larger ones, two for a pound!

There is a old bounder named Blades
Whose favourite pastime's parlour maids;
    Though young chaps and whores,
    And the knot-holes in doors
Are by no means exempt from his raids!

To a virgin, a Malibu hunk,
Explained: "Though at present it's shrunk,
  If you take it in hand,
  You will see it expand
And fill you with wonder, and spunk!"

JOHN SLIM

Said the lad: "Have you heard of Flat Lick?"
And she gave him her answer quite quick:
  Laid him down on his back,
  While she tongued him, full whack,
Assuming his talk was of dick.

She could hardly believe her own eyes,
At this most unexpected surprise:
  The bloke was quite small,
  Barely three-foot-six tall,
But his cock – an incredible size!

There is a young fellow from Crick,
Who performs a spectacular trick:
  He can push his big toes
  Half an inch up his nose –
No, it's nothing to do with his dick!

Since he fought for his Equity card,
So many blue movies have starred
  The man with the cock
  That's as solid as rock,
Though he says it was never that hard!

An excitable fellow, in Colt,
Gave a lady a bit of a jolt;
　　When he saw what she'd got,
　　He rapidly shot
Into bed, into her and his bolt!

JOHN SLIM

There was a mechanic called Tench,
Whose best tool was a sturdy gut-wrench;
　　With this vibrant device
　　He could reach, in a trice,
The innermost parts of a wench.

Said an innocent lad from Caerphilly:
"This question may seem a bit silly,
　　But do girls intend
　　That a blow-job should end
With their teeth coming out on the willy?"

Some cocks weigh no more than an ounce,
And others much larger amounts;
　　But it's not what you've got
　　Be it little or lot –
It's what you do with it that counts!

A long-plonkered fellow called Keith,
Bonks birds, kebab-style, in Blackheath;
　　He makes them form lines,
　　Then takes them in nines –
Best on top, and with eight underneath!

There was an old codger of Poole,
Who was blessed with a very large tool;
   He said: "Don't get me wrong –
   Though it's twelve inches long,
I don't use it much as a rule!'

RON RUBIN

An engaging young filly named Sally,
Who enjoys the occasional dally,
    Will sit on the lap
    Of a well-endowed chap,
And declare: "Ooh, you're right up my alley!"

There was an old cockney called Warner,
Who'd a taste for young feminine fauna;
   He'd buy them pig's ear,
   Then have sex at the rear
Of his shop on the little Jack Horner.

RON RUBIN

A rakish young toff, name of Hal,
Went to Venice and met a nice gal;
    But when he started to fondle her
     Tits in a gondola,
She heaved him into the canal.

RON RUBIN

A randy beachcomber named Keeches,
Spends a lot of his time combing beaches,
   Where he helps maiden aunts
   On and off with their pants,
Whilst they assist him with his breeches.

        "By my girl!" cried a lover named Cecil,
        "Is the place where I'm longing to nestle;
           Nothing else is a patch
           On the neat way we match –
        She's the mortar and I am the pestle!"

The sex-drive of old man McGill,
Offers fortunate ladies a thrill;
   It appears his technique
   Is delightful, unique –
Not unlike an electrical drill.

        A gratified lassie, amazed
        At the size of the prize she'd hand-raised,
           Said: "What do we do
           With it now that it's – oohh,
        That's cheeky, but Heaven be praised!"

That man is undoubtedly rare,
Who can stare at a bare derrière,
   And be so unimpressed
   By Sweet Fanny, undressed,
That his flag doesn't wave in the air!

A bit of a nuisance named Liam,
Said: "The best bits are tits, when you see 'em.
   But they're usually trapped,
    Cupped, wired and strapped –
So I make it my mission to free 'em!"

      The insatiable Acquamarine,
      Has always been terribly keen
         On kissing and wooing,
         Indiscriminate screwing,
      And, well – anything vaguely obscene.

A knight at King Arthur's Round Table,
Felt at jousting he wasn't so able;
   He had so much more fun
    Watching Guinevere's bum
From his hiding-place under the table.

IAN HERBERT

      An observant young chap in the West
      Said: "I've discovered, by personal test,
         That men who make passes
         At girls who wear glasses,
      Have just as much fun as the rest!"

I dislike all this crude notoriety
That I'm getting for my impropriety;
   All that I ever do
   Is what girls ask me to –
I'll admit: I get lots of variety!

There is a young bounder called Ted,
Who lures all sorts of girls into bed;
   Although, by and large,
   He much prefers Marge,
Because Marge is so easy to spread.

     Said Bert: "Let's be wheelbarrow-lovers!"
     As he'd tried it with one or two others;
       But his wife answered: "Bert,
       Is it going to hurt?
     And will we be going past Mother's?"

S & M was his plan but we guess
The less said the better – unless
   He was also turned on
   When he found that she'd gone
To buy him a tie (M & S)!

JOHN SLIM

     She'd been quite impressed with his flock,
     So he promised to show her his cock;
       Imagining sheds
       Full of Rhode Island Reds,
     Poor young Hazel was in for a shock . . .

A well-endowed bounder called Rogers,
Possessed one of the legendary todgers;
   When he ran for the bus,
   It would leap from its truss
And surprise unsuspecting old codgers.

An adventurous chap from East Anstey,
Suggested to his girlfriend, Nancy:
   "Straightforward, or oral,
   Or backwards, or whoral –
I'm game for what tickles your fancy!"

A Scots sailor, christened McPhie,
Spoonerizes embarrassingly;
   He once shouted, "You wanker!"
   Instead of, "Weigh anchor!"
And introduces himself as "PhcMie".

An old lighthouse-keeper from Orme,
Snuggled up to his wife to keep warm;
   She said: "Darling, your cock
   Is like Eddystone Rock,
In its shape and in colour and form!"

A bonny young Scots laddie, built
A bit like a tank in his kilt,
   Complained to his mate:
   "It won't come up straight –
The lass says: "It will and I wilt!"

A girl who went in for a swim,
In the nude, said: "It's great once you're in."
   And the chap with the cock
   Who gave her such a shock,
Said it certainly felt good to him!

In a hardware store, sex-mad young Stu,
Asked the girl working there for a screw;
   She said: "Why not? With pleasure,
   What's more, for good measure,
I'll give you some nuts and bolts too!"

RON RUBIN

What is pinkish and roundish and hairy,
And hangs down from a bush, light and airy;
   Much hidden away
   From the bright light of day,
Beneath a stiff prick? A gooseberry!

A gratified fellow called Rob,
Found a girl on the end of his knob;
   He'd had forty winks,
   And that's when he thinks
She arrived and got on with the job!

JOHN SLIM

A yokel who lives in Devizes,
Has bollocks of differing sizes;
   One, weighing a pound,
   Drags along on the ground.
The other's as small as a fly's is!

"Talk dirty," she begged him, politely,
So he said awful things to her nightly;
   And it's doing the trick
   (She might wear out his prick),
We have never seen granny so sprightly!

Said Wendy the waitress: "I try
Not to keep people waiting, that's why
   I am there double-quick
   When a chap waves his dick
In an effort at catching my eye!"

A guide volunteer named Mark,
Had a todger that glowed in the dark;
   At nightfall, his job
   Was to whip out his knob,
And lead ladies home through the park.

JOHN SLIM

     A lascivious lecher, called Fletcher,
     Was also a talented sketcher
        Of ladies (quite nude)
        He invariably screwed –
     But did they enjoy it? You betcha!

When people could not understand,
Why he had to have sex on demand
   And they said he should purge
   This ridiculous urge,
He told them he'd got it in hand!

     Said a chap with two choppers: "My dear,
     As Nature has not made it clear,
        I really don't know
        Where the second should go –
     Unless it will reach round the rear!"

JOHN SLIM

There was a young fellow named Cass
Whose bollocks were made out of brass;
   When they tinkled together,
    They played "Stormy Weather",
And lightning shot out of his ass!

An expatriate Scotsman in Durham,
Makes the girls in those parts squeal and squir-um;
   He withdraws then lets fly,
    Shouting: "Mud in your eye!"
Which is where he deposits his spur-um!

Miss Muffet slumped back in the corn,
Her clothing all tattered and torn;
   It wasn't a spider
   That sat down beside her,
'Twas Little Boy Blue, with his horn!

      A guardsman who hailed from Glasgow,
      Was asked what he wore down below;
         With a tilt of his kilt,
         He replied: "If tha' wilt –
      Tha' may'st feel for thaself, then tha'lst know!"

There are some things men must not expose,
Which they keep tucked away in their clothes
   And it's thought rude to stare
   At what's bulging there,
Although why this is so, Heaven knows!

      Have you heard of the Giant of Neath,
      Who screws pixies that live on the heath?
         His runcible dong
         Is so terribly long.
      It emerges between their front teeth!

There was a young lady of Chester,
Who fell madly in love with a jester;
   Though her breath came out hotly
   At the sight of his motley,
It was really his wand that impressed her!

There once was a handsome young sheikh,
With a marvellous penile physique;
   Though its length and its weight
   Made it look really great,
He fell woefully short on technique.

There was a young fellow from Juilliard,
With a penis that measured a full yard;
   Girls whispered and leered,
   And most of them cheered
Whenever he ran through the schoolyard!

      A forward young rascal named Farr,
      Had a habit of goosing his Ma;
         "Go and pester your sister,"
         She said, when he kissed her,
      "I've enough trouble coping with Pa!"

James Bond is an agent I've heard
Who boasts he can pull any bird,
   But his date for tonight
   Is a cute transvestite –
I'm sure he'll be shaken not stirred!

JANET SMITH

      I'll admit I impregnated Marge,
      So I do rather feel, by and large,
         Some cash should be tendered
         For services rendered,
      But I can't decide quite what to charge!

Said old Father William: "I'm humble,
And getting too weak for a tumble,
    But produce me a blonde,
    And I'm still not beyond
An attempt at an interesting fumble."

CONRAD AIKEN

A lawyer whose todger extended,
Much further than Nature intended,
    Was sometimes caught short,
    And ran from the court
To be tripped by the tip, and upended!

JOHN SLIM

At the bullfight, José made his bid;
When the maiden agreed he was rid
    Of all inhibitions,
    And despite the conditions
As the crowd yelled, "Olé!" José did!

A young electrician from Distance
Said: "Ma'am, can I be of assistance?"
    But he got quite a shock
    When she took off her frock,
And said: "Will you test my resistance?"

CYRIL BIBBY

A lusty farm lad, for a joke,
Gave the hens in the farmyard a poke;
   But his vice was betrayed
   When the eggs that they laid
Contained nothing but white, with no yoke!

       When God made his prototype Man,
       He mislaid vital parts of the plan;
          And unsightly sections,
          Like bums and erections,
       He ought to improve when he can.

Said an old English gentlemen toff:
"Please, top up your glasses, let's quaff
   To short-skirted joys
   Which enable the boys
To begin where their fathers left off!"

       Beware! There's a devil named Dick,
       Well-endowed with a humungous prick;
          From its tip, like a prism,
          He can shoot enough jism
       To make any poor cocksucker sick.

Queen Mary found Scotsmen are built,
With a definite angular tilt;
   To her regal surprise,
   Every member would rise
Every time she groped under a kilt!

"What a shame!" said a winsome young miss,
"That an organ that brings me such bliss,
   With its delicate touch,
   Should be wasted on such
An unpleasant production as piss!"

ISAAC ASIMOV

     The harlots who come from Devizes,
     Can accommodate cocks of all sizes,
        From one inch to ten –
        Which covers most men –
     Those longer than that receive prizes.

A greengrocer, somewhere near Chard,
Pays double entendres no regard;
    Thus it is that one grapples
    With a sign on his apples
Informing you: "These cox are hard."

JOHN SLIM

    A beefy young copper named Plod,
    Renowned for the size of his rod,
        Attempted to stuff it
        Up Little Miss Muffet –
    The last words she spoke were: "My God!"

Said the passionate Countess of Ewell:
"All the boys want, of course, is my jewel!
    But I make my selection
    By length of erection –
Twelve inches is fine, as a rule!"

    There was a young fellow called Jed,
    Whose cock was the length of the bed;
        Said his girlfriend: "Your prick
        Is too long and too thick –
    Let's decamp to the pictures instead!"

A diminutive maiden named Hilda,
Had a date with a top body-builder;
    He said that he should,
    That he could and he would,
And he did – and it pretty near killed her!

There was a young cad from Belgrave,
Who kept a dead whore in a cave;
   He said: "I admit
   I'm a bit of a shit,
But think of the money I'll save."

A sturdy young fellow from Poole,
Had been blessed with an enormous tool;
   When fully extended,
   The thing only ended
A couple of miles short of Goole!

There was a young man of Dumfries,
Who said to his girl: "If you please,
   It would give me great bliss
   If, while playing with this,
You would pay some attention to these!"

His neighbours all looked quite askance a lot,
At a passionate fellow called Lancelot;
   Whenever he'd pass
   A presentable lass,
The front of his pants would advance a lot!

There was a young man from Poughkeepsie,
Who, whenever he got slightly tipsy,
    Would whip out his tool,
    And attack, like a fool,
Any girl who was breasty and hipsy.

ISAAC ASIMOV

There was a young woman of Sydney,
Who could take it clear up to the kidney;
    But the thrust of Alphonse
    Barely reached to her mons –
So he left her unsatisfied, didney?

ISAAC ASIMOV

A psychiatrist said: "It's no matter,
That my husband's as mad as a hatter.
    There are certain psychoses
    That bring sex in large doses –
My husband, you see, is a satyr!"

We all laughed when a fellow named Ollie,
Once swore he would screw a young dolly;
    "For twelve hours I'll engage her!"
    And he laid down his wager,
We all laughed but he did it, by golly!

An Olympian lecher was Zeus:
Always playing around fast and loose,
   With one hand in the bodice
   Of some likely young goddess,
And the other preparing to goose.

ISAAC ASIMOV

      A friend has an end to his member,
      That, once seen, one would always remember;
         The size of this knob's
         Much too big for most gobs,
      So cock-sucking is off the agenda!

The risks that he took were quite minimal.
The results he achieved were subliminal:
   Stole Viagra; he'll find
   The police have in mind
To look for a new hardened criminal!

7.

The Trombonist Called Grange, the Scandal of Handel, and Other Tales from the Arts

If you find for your verse there's no call,
And you can't afford paper at all,
   For the poet, true born,
   However forlorn,
There is always the lavatory wall!

      Far removed from the girls of Pirelli,
      Are the ladies of S Botticelli:
         Each with porcelain skin
         And a pert little chin,
      And erogenous botti and belli!

A playwright, to vulgar inclined,
Wrote a drama more gross than refined,
   With words, all four-letter
   (Hips, lips, tits and better),
Like those that have just crossed your mind!

      A short-sighted actor, enraged,
      Muttered thus to an actress, on stage:
         "When I fell for you,
         I believed fifty-two
      Was the size of your tits, not your age!"

An erotica writer, called May,
Dreamt up hot fantasies every day;
   Though her fingers ignored
   Her computer keyboard
As her clit became quite worn away!

CAROL ANNE DAVIS

A painter of Pop Art, named Jock,
Decorated each canvas to shock;
   Outsize genitalia
   Gave onlookers heart failure,
But the critics decreed: "Poppycock!"

      An artist, named Sammy McHugh,
      Once painted his organ bright blue;
         When he'd finished his work,
         He remarked, with a smirk:
      "Now I've got a reply for 'What's new?'"

A crooner, who lived in West Shore,
Caught both of his balls in a door;
   Now his mezzo soprano
   Is rather piano,
Though he was a loud basso before!

      A blonde woodwind player, named June,
      Had arrived at rehearsals by noon,
         When a man in the band
         Put his flute in her hand,
      It soon changed to a contra bassoon.

A lady, removing her scanties,
Heard them crackle electrical shanties;
   Said her husband: "My dear,
   I very much fear
You're suffering from amps in your panties!"

There was a young Scot named McAmiter,
Who bragged of excessive diameter;
   Though it wasn't the size
   That brought tears to their eyes,
But the rhythm – iambic hexameter!

Charlotte Bronte said: "Wow, sister, what a man!
He laid me face down on the ottoman:
   Now don't you, or Emily,
   Go telling the femily –
But he smacked me upon my bare bottom, Anne!"

VICTOR GRAY

A yogi, from far-off Beirut,
For women did not care a hoot,
   But his organ would stand
   In a manner quite grand
When a snake-charmer played on his flute.

A lonely old maid named Loretta,
Sent herself an anonymous letter,
   Quoting Ellis on sex,
   And Oedipus Rex,
And exclaimed: "I already feel better!"

There once was a great prima donna,
Whose co-star leaped madly upon her;
   "Let's do it!" he cried.
   "Sure thing!" she replied,
"But right here, onstage, I don't wanna!"

A young ballerina called Sally,
Badly wanted to dance in the ballet;
   She got roars of applause
   When she kicked off her drawers
For her hair and her bush didn't tally!

     A talented painter, called Duff,
     Hired a model to pose in the buff;
        She had such a huge ass,
        He discovered, alas,
     That his canvas was not big enough.

A flatulent nun of Hawaii,
One Easter Eve supped on papaya,
   Then honoured the Passover
   By turning her arse over,
And obliging with Handel's *Messiah!*

      The best way to read Conan Doyle,
      Is sitting astride Katie Boyle;
         When she cries: "PTO!"
         That's the moment to go –
      There are some things from which I recoil.

When Angelico worked in Cerise,
For the Angel he painted his niece;
   In a heavenly trance,
   He pulled off her pants
And erected a fine altar-piece!

A Victorian gent said: "This dance,
The Can-Can, which we've got from France,
   Fills me with disgust;
   It generates lust –
You must see it when you have the chance!"

FRANK RICHARDS

      When requested to pose in the nude,
      And not wishing to seem like a prude,
         She gave a small cough
         As she took her clothes off –
      This story to be continued...

A Hollywood star, named De Niro,
Who had never been cast as the hero,
   Decided to start
   To build up his part –
Now a porn star, his cock weighs a kilo!

      There was a young man in Havana,
      Fucked a girl on a player pianna;
         At the height of their fever,
         Her ass hit the lever –
      And, oh yes – he has no banana!

An unfortunate vocalist, Springer,
Got his testicles caught in the wringer;
   He hollered with pain,
   As they rolled down the drain:
"There goes my career as a singer."

      A clever young chap from Beirut,
      Played his penis as one might a flute;
         Till he met a sad eunuch,
         Who lifted his tunic,
      And said: "Look, my instrument's mute."

As Apollo pursued her, the fair
Lovely Daphne vanished in thin air;
   He found but a shrub
   With rough bark on the hub,
And not even a knot-hole to spare.

A TV presenter named Herschel,
Harbours habits a tad controversial;
   While he is out wooing,
   Whatever he's doing,
At ten he inserts his commercial.

An eccentric young poet named Brown,
Lifted up his embroiderèd gown
      To look for his peter,
      And beat it to meter
But fainted when none could be found.

When they named an inflatable vest,
After busty screen goddess, Mae West,
   She said: "I should be feted
   For the men that I've dated
And not just for the size of my chest!"

JANET SMITH

For sculpture that's really first class,
You need form, composition and mass;
      To do a good Venus,
      Just leave off the penis,
And concentrate more on the ass!

In the soap-operas seen in Gomorrah,
The heroine wakes up in horrah
   To find that a prick;
   Nearly three inches thick,
Is halfway up... tune in tomorrah!

A talented pianist named Liszt,
Could perform with one hand, while he pissed;
   And, as he grew older,
   His technique became bolder,
And he often jacked off in his fist.

      An old music-lover of Mecca,
      Has discovered a record from Decca,
         Which he twirls on his thumb
         (Such eccentrics are dumb)
      While he needles the disc with his pecca.

Said a lady who sat on a flute:
"At last! I've the means to refute
   The unkindly aspersions
   Of those whose assertions
Imply that I don't give a hoot!"

JOHN SLIM

      Said a slant-eyed young jade of Japan:
      "I must study under Paul Gauguin!"
         Though he taught her at first,
         Soon their places reversed,
      Whence she soon became Yin, and he Yang.

Regardez-vous Toulouse Lautrec,
Though at first glance an ambulant wreck,
   He could fuck once a week
   À la manière antique,
And now and again *à la Grecque.*

A naturist chap named O'Neil,
Fancied playing the old campanile;
   He made the gong bong
   With the end of his dong –
Now he's struggling to get it to heal.

A clever young fellow named Saul,
Could do marvellous tricks with each ball:
   He could stretch them, and snap them,
   And juggle, and clap them,
Which earned him the plaudits of all.

A randy composer, they tell,
Found that screwing to music was hell;
   Everything went just fine
   Till he got out of time,
And cried: "This isn't Bach – it's Ravel!"

Whilst Theocritus guarded his flock,
He composed in the shade of a rock;
   It is said that his Muse
   Was the best of the ewes,
With a bum like a pink hollyhock.

A circus performer named Dick,
Has perfected a wonderful trick:
   With a safe for protection,
   He'll contrive an erection,
And balance himself on his prick.

An unsatisfied actress from Crewe,
Justly said, as the Bishop withdrew:
   "The vicar was quicker,
   And thicker, and slicker,
And four inches longer than you!"

A well-known TV Chat Show host,
Has decided the guests he likes most
   Are celebrity gobs
   Who'll accommodate knobs
Not unlike the one he's proud to boast!

A conductor, performing in Rome,
Had a quaint way of driving things home:
   Whoever he climbed,
   Had to keep her tail timed
To the beat of his old metronome.

A circus performer named Spitz,
Was inclined to quite passionate fits;
   His main pleasure in life
   Was to suck off his wife,
As he swung by his knees from her tits.

   A theatre-goer named Walls,
   Seemed possessed of inadequate balls,
      Till one night, at the Strand,
      He did manage a stand,
   So he tossed himself off in the stalls.

The cross-eyed, old artist, MacNeff,
Was colour-blind, palsied and deaf;
   When he asked to be touted,
   The critics all shouted:
"This is art – with a capital F!"

   A musical condom has been
   Introduced on the love-making scene;
      It sees you all right
      With All Through The Night,
   And stands up for God Save The Queen!

JOHN SLIM

A young fiddler playing first fiddle,
Asked his soloist friend: "Do you diddle?"
   She replied: "Yes, I do,
   But prefer to with two –
I enjoy it much more in the middle."

"For the tenth time, dull Daphnis," said Chloe,
"You have told me my bosom is snowy;
    You've composed much fine verse on
    Each part of my person,
Now do something – there's a good boy!"

A musician in gay Montebello
Will amuse herself playing the cello;
    No, not a solo –
    She employs, as a bow,
The long dong of a sturdy young fellow.

A male ballet dancer wears gear,
That intrigues from the front and the rear;
When you view from the back,
You see right up his crack,
Yet his bollocks are never that clear.

There was a young poet whose sex,
Was aroused by aesthetic effects;
Marvell's The Garden
Gave him a hard-on
And he came during Oedipus Rex.

A musical maiden from Frome,
Allowed a friend's fingers to roam;
He taught her the score,
Then gave an encore
On her other erogenous zone.

CYRIL BIBBY

While viewing a painting of Venus,
A young student added a penis;
He had to erase it:
He'd been asked to praise it –
At least he found out what a paean is!

A fortunate fellow of Warwick,
Had good reason to feel euphoric;
He could, by election,
Have triune erection:
Ionic, Corinthian, and Doric.

There was a young lady called Gloria,
Who was had by Sir Gerald Du Maurier,
    Another six men,
    Sir Gerald, again,
And the band at the Waldorf Astoria!

The desirable young Lady Chatterley,
Took an interest in shrubbery latterly;
  When her gardener said:
  "You look gorgeous in bed!"
She replied: "Sir, you really do flatter me!"

LES WILKIE

When a stand-up comedian tried,
To tell anecdotes re: his new bride,
    "His stand-up," she said,
    "Needs a hand-up in bed,
So – let's leave smutty stories aside!"

A famous theatrical actress,
Performs best in the role of malefactress;
  Her private life's pure
  Even when she's on tour,
Save a scandal or two (just for practice).

An Italian youngster named Ringer
Who was screwing an opera singer;
    Cried out, with a grin:
    "Mamma mia, it's in!"
Said she: "You mean that's not your finger?"

A guitarist by the name of Renato,
Made love somewhat *tempo rubato;*
   "At the rate that you strum,"
   Said his girl, "I won't come –
Perhaps you should use some *vibrato?*"

RON RUBIN

   "Do you know," asked a punter called Dai,
   "'I'm in Love with a Wonderful Guy'?"
     The pianist replied,
      Without missing his stride:
   "I suppose, ducks, then this is goodbye?"

RON RUBIN

A curvaceous dancer, called Anne,
Did flirtatious things with her fan;
   As it waved in and out,
   She left no one in doubt
She'd acquired an all-over tan!

ELEANOR ROGERS

   A lady guitarist of Bude
   Was asked: "Can you play 'In the Mood'?"
     She replied: "Why not? Sure!"
     But her hearing was poor,
   And she stripped off and strummed – in the nude!

RON RUBIN

Chopin – let's just call him Fred, –
Eloped with George Sand to the Med;
   (I hasten to mensh
   That George S was a wench,
In case some dear reader's misled.)

RON RUBIN

An organist, playing in York,
Had a prick that could grip a small fork;
   And, between obligatos,
   He'd munch on tomatoes –
It's either the truth or just talk!

The hen-night magician thought quick
When something went wrong with his trick;
   Coloured hankies and doves
   Were eluding his gloves,
So he whipped out his show-stopping dick!

The pairing of Tom and Louise,
Do an act in the nude, on their knees;
   They crawl down the aisle
   As they screw doggy-style,
And the orchestra plays Kilmer's "Trees".

Four quadruplets in the Bahamas
Frequented dance-halls in pyjamas;
   Being fondled all summer
   By bass, sax, and drummer –
It's a miracle they're not all mammas!

"We've a new French chanteuse," grumbled Lars,
Whose repertoire's really too sparse,
   And her pitching is poor –
   But the band all adore
The way that the girl rolls her Rs!"

RON RUBIN

A voluptuous dancer from Wheeling,
Always danced with such exquisite feeling;
   There was barely a sound
   For some miles around,
Save for fly-buttons hitting the ceiling.

If you can't get it up, here's the answer:
Spend some time with an exotic dancer;
   Her magnificent tits
   Plus her jiggly bits
Will soon give you a lump in your pants, sir!

The composer, George Frideric Handel,
Whose sexual life was a scandal,
   Grew red in the face
   When he wrote figured bass,
So he buggered himself with a candle.

There's going to be a divorce:
Their marriage has wavered off course
   Since she found hubby sunk
   To his bollocks in spunk
Up the rear of a pantomime horse!

Pinocchio's never found why,
Whenever he gives sex a try,
   The lady just goes
   And sits on his nose,
And gasps: "Little bastard, now – lie!"

JOHN SLIM

There's a juggling clown who has shown,
A sexual flair all his own:
   On his cock's a red nose,
   And he humps while he throws
Five balls in the air – two his own!

JOHN SLIM

      There was a trombonist, called Grange,
      Who had an incredible range:
         Schoolgirls, stenographers,
         Nuns, choreographers,
      And sometimes boy scouts for a change.

    RON RUBIN

Those men who are born under Taurus
Are attracted to girls of the chorus –
   They go on to excursions
   In varied perversions,
But, forget it – the details would bore us!

A sexy young dancer, named Sally,
Was performing one night in the ballet;
  To tumultuous applause
  (She'd forgotten her drawers),
She displayed a fine view of her valley.

There's a randy *tenore robusto*
Who pursues the sopranos *con gusto;*
  In the last act of Faust,
  (He'll admit he was soused),
He manhandled the diva's *bel busto!*

During sex, Mary's moans were harmonic,
From High C down by chords to the tonic;
   So John felt it unsordid
   To have them recorded
In sound that was stereophonic.

ISAAC ASIMOV

Two piano duettists, from Cheam,
Who will even make love as a team:
   One aft and one frontal,
   With strokes contrapuntal –
Have developed a fucking good theme.

The new cinematic emporium,
Is not just a super-sensorium,
   But a highly effectual
   Heterosexual
Mutual masturbatorium.

A talented cellist in Rio,
Was seducing a lady named Cleo;
   As she lowered her panties,
   She said: "No *andantes* –
I want this *allegro con brio*!"

A poet, whose verses inclined,
To the rude and the raucous, opined:
   "Abusing my muse
   Is not what I choose –
But I do have the filthiest mind!"

While Titian was mixing rose madder,
His model reclined on a ladder;
   Her position, to Titian,
   Suggested coition,
So he shinned up the ladder and had 'er.

Young Jane was a lollapalooza,
Although no-one could manage to use her;
   She wouldn't screw with them
   Except to the rhythm
Of the marches of John Philip Souza.

ISAAC ASIMOV

A young woman from South Carolina,
Had placed fiddle strings 'cross her vagina;
    With the proper sized cocks,
    What was sex became Bach's
"Toccata and Fugue in D Minor".

ISAAC ASIMOV

Does Penis Van Lesbian strike
A chord, as a name folks might like
    For an actor, or will
    You opt for the thrill
Of just being plain Dick Van Dyke?

JOHN SLIM

It wasn't the thing one expects
In a bookshop: by craning our necks
    We found on a shelf,
    Under Do-it-Yourself,
That helpful small tome Joy of Sex.

JOHN SLIM

A young violinist named Biddle,
Played exceedingly well on the fiddle;
    Yet, twixt women and art,
    'Twas the girls won his heart,
Hand down and hands up – and hands middle.

ISAAC ASIMOV

8.
Fitzpatrick, Fitzgerald and Me – Such Gay Company!

There was a young Turkish cadet,
And this is the damnedest one yet –
 His tool was so long,
 And incredibly strong,
He could bugger six Greeks, *en brochette*!

Three sweet little boys from the ballet,
Had a lovely night out at the Palais;
 But the end of their day,
 I am sorry to say,
Was spent with three burgers from Calais.

A classical chap from Victoria,
In a post-alcoholic euphoria,
 Was discovered, one day,
 In a club for the gay,
Immersed in an *ars amatoria*.

There once was a sinister ottoman,
To the fair sex I fear he was not a man;
 He evaded the charms
 Of all feminine arms –
Quite frankly, he said: "I'm a bottom man!"

A lesbian lady, named Annie,
Wished to be much less girlie, more manny;
 So she whittled a pud
 Out of gnarly old wood,
And let it protrude from her cranny.

There was a young bride named laVerne,
Who found she'd a great deal to learn:
   The man she had wed
   Liked to take chaps to bed,
And she didn't know *which* way to turn!

       Well buggered's a chap called Delpasse,
       By the rest of the lads in his class;
          He insists, with a yawn:
          "Now the novelty's gone,
       This is simply a pain in the ass!"

There was a young fellow called Chubb,
Who joined a smart Buggery Club;
   But his parts were so small,
   He was no use at all,
And they promptly refunded his sub.

       There was a young man, of Wood's Hole,
       Who had an affair with a mole;
          A bit of a nancy,
          He did rather fancy
       Himself in the dominant role.

A whore, for a bit of a joke,
Wore an invisibility cloak,
   So that tricks couldn't see
   If a she or a he
Was the subject of such a good poke!

When Santa gets bored in his Grotto,
He doesn't play bingo, or lotto;
　　He sits on a shelf,
　　And toys with an elf –
"Sod this for a lark!" is his motto.

Said Nelson, at his most la-di-da-di:
"I am sorry if I'm rather tardy,
　　But I'm in a dilemma:
　　Should I bugger Emma,
Or screw the delectable Hardy?"

A CINNA

There were two horny brothers named Luntz,
Who buggered each other at once;
　　When asked to account
　　For this intricate mount,
They said: "Assholes are tighter than cunts."

A big Catholic layman named Fox,
Makes his living by sucking off cocks;
　　In spells of depression,
　　He goes to confession,
And jacks off the priest in his box.

A dandy so much oversexed,
He is easily fretted and vexed;
　　When out with a chap,
　　Barely holds himself back,
Crying: "Turn over, bud, my turn next"

A gay soccer spectator from Wix,
Thought rugger might offer new tricks;
   He didn't go much
   For kicking for touch,
But fancied the touching for kicks.

CYRIL MOUNTJOY

King Richard, in one of his rages,
Forsook his good lady for ages,
   And rested in bed
   With a good book instead,
Or, preferably, one of the pages.

A B HALL

There was a young fellow named Howell,
Who buggered himself with a trowel;
    The triangular shape
    Was conducive to rape,
And was easily cleaned with a towel.

A native of Havre de Grace,
When tired of cunt thought: "Try arse."
   He unfolded his plan
   To another young man,
Who said, in collusion: "My arse!"

"I'll do it for Art – I'm no prude!"
Said he, as he posed in the nude;
    But, on viewing his ass,
    The entire fairy class
Decided it ought to be screwed.

When the Nazis landed in Crete,
Young harlots worked hard to compete
   With the many Storm Troopers
   Who were using their poopers
For other things than to excrete.

A salacious old chap from Estretto,
Buggered every young man in the ghetto;
    He once had his hose in
    A musician composing,
Who said: "Not so slow – *allegretto*!"

A dexterous chap of Madras,
Used to stretch himself out on the grass,
  And found it no trouble,
  To bend himself double,
And stick his prick up his own ass!

A whimsical arab from Aden,
With his masculine member well laden,
  Cried: "Nuptial joy,
  When shared with a boy,
Is much better than melon or maiden!"

A promiscuous fairy named Bates,
Takes out lots of young fellows on dates;
  With *his* hands on *their* hips,
  He'll apply his hot lips
To their phalluses, testes and nates.

What a bounder is Mr Magoo!
There is nothing the fellow won't screw;
  Old Duchesses, cooks,
  They are all on his books,
And he dabbles in sodomy too!

A lesbian said: "It's a shock to me!
How thoughtful and kind can a doctor be!
  He says he'll extend a
  Help to my gender –
The process is called 'strapacoctomy'!"

JOHN SLIM

A randy bisexual punk,
Who screwed the closed orders when drunk,
    Said: "I like having fun –
    If there's none with a nun,
There's a bonk in a bunk with a monk!"

A dashing young fellow, McBride,
Preferred his cocks long, thick and wide;
    But he never rejected
    Anything that erected,
For "Peter is peter!" he cried.

"At a séance," said a fellow named Post,
"I was being sucked off by a ghost;
    Someone switched on the lights –
    Blow me! There, in gauze tights,
On his knees, was Elias, mine host!"

The priests at the temple of Isis,
Used to offer up amber and spices;
    At the back of the shrine,
    They enjoyed sixty-nine,
And some other unmentionable vices.

A Roman of old named Horatio,
Was particularly fond of fellatio;
    He kept a long list
    Of each penis he'd kissed,
And he called it his cock-sucking ratio.

Pity poor Robinson Crusoe:
He hadn't a woman to screw, so
   He'd sit on a rock
   And fondle his cock,
Or get his Man Friday to do so.

Reminisced bounder Baron McFiggle,
With an almost hysterical giggle:
   "Late last night I was sick
   With delight when my prick
Felt young Tarquin's posterior wriggle!"

Said a lesbian lady: "It's sad,
But of all the good times I have had,
   None gave me the thrill
   Of true rapture, until
I found out how to be a tribad."

     There was an old bugger of Brienz,
     The length of whose cock was immense;
       With one swerve he could plug
       A chap's bottom in Zug,
     And a kitchen-maid's cunt in Coblenz.

A fussy and fashionable nance,
Who responded to any advance,
   Would, rather than strip,
   Just let everything slip
Through a hole in the seat of his pants.

     There was a young man from Nantucket,
     Who had such a big cock he could suck it;
       When he glanced in the glass,
       He caught sight of his ass,
     And broke his neck trying to fuck it.

There was a hermaphrodite kid,
Made a pass at a man in Madrid;
   "Why, you son of a maggot,
   Do you think *I'm* a faggot?
Just go fuck yourself!" So he did.

There was a young man who said: "Why
Can't I bugger myself, if I'm spry?
   If I put my mind to it,
   I'm sure I can do it –
And you never can tell till you try."

      A parson who lived outside Bourne,
      Looked down on all women with scorn;
         No chap's plump white bum
         Could inspire him to come,
      But an old sod's piles gave him the horn.

A tight-fisted chap from Delray,
Who had buggered his pater one day,
   Said: "I do enjoy rather
   To stuff it up father –
He's clean, and there's nothing to pay!"

      There was a young Sapphic named Anna,
      Who stuffed her friend's cunt with banana,
         Which she sucked for a bit
         From her partner's hot slit,
      In a most approved lesbian manner.

A young man who hailed from Balbriggan,
Went to sea as a respite from frigging,
   But on the first morn,
   In the Cape of Good Horn,
He buggered the mate in the rigging.

Thus spake the King of Siam:
"For women I don't care a damn;
   But a fat-bottomed boy
   Is my pride and my joy –
They call me a bugger: I am!"

"Indeed," quoth the King of Siam,
"For cunts I just don't give a damn;
   They haven't the grip,
   Nor the velvety tip,
Nor the scope of the asshole of man."

Then up spake the Bey of Algiers,
And said to his harem: "My dears,
   You may think it odd of me,
   But I've given up sodomy –
Tonight there'll be fucking!" (Loud cheers.)

Then up spake the young King of Spain:
"To fuck and to bugger is pain;
   But it's not *infra dig*
   On occasion, to frig,
And I do it again and again."

Then up spake a Hindu mahout,
And said: "What's this blithering about?
   Why, I shoot my spunk
   Up an elephant's trunk!"
(Cries of "Shame! He's a shit! Throw him out!")

There was a young guy from Reliance,
Who fucked his own ass in defiance
   Not only of custom
   And morals, dad-bust him,
But most of the known laws of science!

      A floozie from Frankfurt's grown fond,
      Of a lad who's limp-wristed and blond;
         Says Mary: "I'm wary,
         I know he's a fairy,
      But he does have a way with his wand!"

Some blokes are incredibly hairy,
And the size of their cocks is quite scary;
   Though you'd never know
   At the club whose motto
Insists: Welcome! Eat, drink, and be Mary!

      A dirty old sod, from Cadiz,
      Whose vice is not nice is a whizz
         At unnatural events;
         When he hangs round the Gents,
      They call him a bugger. He is!

      JOHN SLIM

There are several good reasons why Walter,
Is determined that he'll never alter:
   Afternoons that he spends
   With unusual friends,
And weekends clad in saddle and halter!

A kinky old cowboy, called Marriott,
Likes to whip plump young rumps with his lariat:
   "I'll render quite tender
   With my lasso so slender,
Any old Tom, Dick, or Harriet!"

RON RUBIN

There was an old bugger from Poole
With a varicose vein in his tool;
   In attempting to come
   Up another chap's bum,
It went bang, and he felt *such* a fool!

Such an interesting tribe are the Sweenies:
World-renowned for the length of their peenies;
   Though the hair on their balls
   Sweeps the floors of their halls,
They don't bother with women, the meanies!

A prince, with a temper (outrageous),
Filled his palace to bursting with pages
   That were used for much buggery,
   And other skulduggery,
Though he castrated some in his rages.

Said a young Irish guardsman from Buckingham:
"As for ladies I'm not against fucking 'em;
   Although when I meet boys,
   Hubba! How I enjoys
Licking their dickies and sucking 'em!"

A harlot (and gourmet) named Hayes,
Said: "I'm happy to give my guys lays,
    If they bring vaseline
    Or just plain magarine,
But I hate wasting good mayonnaise!"

A fellow from Chicopee, Mass.,
Rejected another man's pass;
    He felt some attraction,
    But recalled that the action
Might well prove a pain in the ass!

ISAAC ASIMOV

A young public school chap named Teddy,
With the juniors used to go steady;
    Till the nosey old Head
    Caught the bounder in bed
With a fourth-former, upturned and ready!

An impossible poser, called Dan,
Beguiled a young thing from Cwmbran;
    The one common factor
    That seemed to attract her
Was... both of them loved the same man!

JOHN SLIM

There was a young actor named Mallory,
Who gobbled his boss in the gallery;
    He agreed, with some wit:
    "Yes, I may be a shit –
But look at the size of my salary!"

Said a shrewd businessman from Belgrade,
Whose mind dwelt on commerce and trade:
    "I will suck, without charge,
    Any cock, if it's large –
If it's not I expect to be paid!"

Recent callers on kinky Miss Fay,
Her neighbours believe, must be gay,
    For none, when they call,
    Use the front door at all –
But always go in the back way!

An effete aesthete, frilly Fred,
To a fruity young friend sadly said:
   "When I woke up last night,
   Just imagine my fright
When I found a nude girl in my bed!"

Fitzpatrick, Fitzgerald and me,
   Are such frightfully gay company;
     Fitz P fits Fitz G,
     And Fitz G fits Fitz P,
   And, yes – each of those Fitzes fits me!

A youth who seduced a poor lighterman,
Said: "I'd much sooner fuck him than fight a man,
   And, although, sir, I find
   You a very good grind,
I must tell you I've had a much tighter man."

9.

The Farter of La Plata and Others of Her Ilk

There was a young man from Australia,
Who painted his arse like a dahlia;
   The colour was fine,
   Likewise the design;
The aroma? Ah, that was a failure.

      Said a printer, pretending to wit:
      "There are certain rude words we omit –
         It would sully our art
         To include the word f---,
      And we seldom, if ever, say s---!"

There was an old man from Bhoghat,
Whose arse cheeks were terribly fat;
   They had to be parted
   Whenever he farted,
And propped wide apart when he shat.

      That delightful bartender, at Sweeney's,
      Is renowned for his cocktails and wienies;
         But I thought him uncouth
         To gulp gin and vermouth,
      Chill the glasses, and piddle martinis!

Said the Duchess of Chester, at tea:
"Now, young man. do you fart when you pee?"
  I replied with quick wit:
  "Do you belch when you shit?"
She conceded. One-nothing to me!

There was an amazing old wizard
Who got a fierce pain in his gizzard;
  So he drank wind and snow
  At some fifty-below,
And farted a forty-day blizzard!

There is a young maiden of Florence,
Who is looked on with general abhorrence;
   In an amorous crush,
   Her poor bladder will flush,
And the stuff tumbles out in great torrents.

       A flatulent Roman, named Titus,
       Was taken with sudden colitis;
          And the venerable Forum
          Lost most of its quorum,
       As he farted up half of the situs.

There was an old sod of Calcutta,
Who greased up his asshole with butter;
   Instead of the roar
   He had heard there before,
Came a soft, oleaginous mutter.

       There was a young fellow named Bart,
       Who strained every shit through a fart;
          Each finely formed turd
          Was the absolute word
       In this deft and most intricate art.

An accomplished old sailor from Wales,
Was that good urinating in gales;
   He could piss in a jar
   From the top-gallant spar
Without ever wetting the sails.

There was a fat lady of Ryde,
Whose shoelaces once came untied;
 She didn't dare stoop
 For fear she would poop,
And she cried and she cried and she cried.

A cabbie who drives in Biarritz,
Once frightened a fare into fits;
 When reproved for a fart,
 He said: "Be of good heart –
When I break wind I usually shits!"

There was a young lady of Purdbright,
Who never could quite get her turd right;
 She'd go to the closet,
 And leave a deposit,
Like a mouse or a bat or a bird might.

There was a young man of Rangoon
Whose farts could be heard on the moon;
 When you didn't expect 'em,
 They burst from his rectum,
With the force of a raging typhoon.

An eager young Royal Marine,
Who tried to fart God Save The Queen,
 Got to the soprano,
 When out shot the guano,
And his breeches weren't fit to be seen.

There was a young man named McBride,
Who could fart anytime that he tried;
  In a contest he blew
  Seven thousand and two,
But then shit and was disqualified.

There was a young man of St Just,
Who ate loaves of bread till he bust;
  It wasn't the crumb,
  For that passed through his bum –
No, what buggered him up was the crust.

There was an old man of Madrid,
Who went to an auction to bid;
  In the first lot they sold,
  Was an ancient commode –
God! The smell when they lifted the lid!

The ghost of a long-dead old dean,
Breaks wind just behind the rood screen;
  The choir is struck dumb,
  Not a soul sees him come,
But everyone knows where he's been.

A young man from the banks of the Po,
Found his cock had elongated so,
  When he had a pee,
  It wasn't just he
But most of his neighbours who'd know.

There was a young fellow called Shit,
A name he disliked quite a bit;
   So he changed it to Shite –
   A step in the right
Direction, one has to admit!

VICTOR GRAY

There is a young man who prefers,
Having sex with unusual birds;
   The rarer the species,
   And the fuller the faeces
The better – that guy loves his turds!

There was a young lady whose joys,
Were achieved with incomparable poise;
   She achieved an orgasm
   With barely a spasm,
And could fart without making much noise.

    There was an old duffer named Droop,
    Who had lost all control of his poop;
       One evening at supper,
       His wife said: "Now, Tupper,
    Stop making that noise with your soup!"

There was a young chap named McFee,
Who was stung on the balls by a bee;
   He made mountains of money
   By oozing pure honey
Every time he attempted to pee!

    There was an old woman named Dottie,
    Who remarked as she straddled her potty:
       "It isn't polite
       To do this in sight,
    But then, who am I to be snotty?"

There was a young man from Montmartre,
Who was famed, far and wide, for his fart;
   When they cried: "What a noise!"
   He replied, with great poise:
"When I fart, sirs, I fart from the heart."

There was an old fellow named Bill,
Who swallowed an atomic pill;
   His navel corroded,
   His asshole exploded,
And they found both his nuts in Brazil.

There was a young man of St James,
Who indulged in the silliest games:
   He ignited the rim
   Of his grandmother's quim,
And guffawed as she pissed out the flames.

There was a young lady of Dexter,
Whose husband invariably vexed her,
   For, whenever they'd start,
   He'd persistently fart
With a blast that damn nearly de-sexed her!

Though flushing is vital for loos,
The stalls in the Gents don't amuse;
   What kind of a swine'll
   Design a urinal
That pisses all over your shoes?

JOHN SLIM

There was a young fellow from Sparta,
A really magnificent farter,
   Fuelled by one single bean,
   He'd fart God Save The Queen –
Also Beethoven's Moonlight Sonata.

He could vary, with proper persuasion,
His fart to suit any occasion;
   He could sound like a flute,
   Or a lark, or a lute,
This amazing, fartistic Caucasian.

He was great in the Christmas Cantata,
He could double-stop fart the Toccata;
   He'd boom from his ass
   Bach's B-Minor Mass,
And, in counterpoint, La Traviata.

Spurred on by a very large wager,
With an envious German named Bager,
   He proceeded to fart
   The complete oboe part
Of a Haydn's Octet in B-Major.

The selection was tough, I admit,
But it did not dismay him a bit;
   Then, with arse held aloft,
    He suddenly coughed –
And collapsed in a shower of shit.

His bunghole was flown back to Sparta,
Where they buried the rest of our farter;
   With a gravestone of turds,
   Thus inscribed with the words:
"To the Fine Art of Farting – A Martyr."

There was an old harlot who farted
As soon as the action had started;
   The rasp from her rump
    made most poor buggers jump –
And before they'd arrived they departed!

A naturist rambler, named Ron,
Walked in nothing but boots and a thong;
   Over stiles, arse in air,
   Is apparently where
The remark "Hello cheeky!" came from.

There was a young fellow of Chislehurst,
Who could not urinate till he'd whistle first;
    One evening, last June,
    He lost track of the tune –
Dum-dee-dee-dum-dee-dum... and his bladder burst!

There was a young fellow of Kent,
Who had a peculiar bent:
    He collected the turds
    Of unusual birds,
And consumed them for lunch, during Lent.

An old, irresponsible bloke,
Who had picked up a tart for a poke;
    On removing her pants,
    Fucked her into a trance,
And then shit in her shoes, for a joke.

A sword-eater, working in Kent,
Had swallowed a sword which was bent;
    As the crowd stood to cheer,
    It emerged from his rear,
Which wasn't at all his intent!

MARIAN SWINGER

An ingenious inventor named Blend,
Made a synthetic arse for a friend;
    But the friend quickly found
    The construction unsound:
It was simply a bother – no end!

The loudest fart ever recorded –
Brother John's, on a plane, as he boarded,
    De-waxed the crew's ears,
    Then drowned all the cheers
Of the passengers as they applauded.

JOHN SLIM

On American freeways, the art
Is to know what the signposts impart;
    Gas Food simply means
    They will sell you baked beans,
For you to convert to a fart.

JOHN SLIM

There are suddenly no signs at all,
Of flies on the dining-room wall;
    It shows we were right
    Putting buckets of shite
In the sitting-room, kitchen and hall.

JOHN SLIM

A poor constipated old bloke,
So blocked up, don't laugh – it's no joke,
   Emitted a blast
   That left listeners aghast,
And yet nothing emerged but some smoke.

There was a young man from the coast,
Who received a small parcel by post;
   It contained, so I heard,
   A triangular turd,
And the balls of his grandfather's ghost!

An elderly spinster, Miss Snood,
Is so much of a prissy old prude:
   That she pulls down the blind
   When she's changing her mind,
Lest libidinous eyes should intrude!

There was a young girl of La Plata,
Who was widely renowned as a farter;
   Her deafening reports
   At the Argentine Sports,
Made her much in demand as a starter.

There was a fat fellow from Stroud,
Who could fart unbelievably loud;
   When he let go a big 'un,
   Dogs were deafened in Wigan,
And window panes cracked at St Cloud!

Said the Duke to the Duchess of Avery,
With abandon that teetered on bravery:
   "You've been sitting on *Punch*
   Since, oh, long before lunch –
Might I have it before it's unsavoury?"

Substantial amounts of such verse,
About predilections quite perverse,
   Is scatological,
   Gynaecological
Bullshit. And often far worse!

"This has been such a marvellous day,"
Yawned Her Ladyship Douglas-MacKay:
  "Three blackberry tarts,
  At least fifty farts,
Several shits, and a bloody good lay!"

There was a young artist called Saint
Who swallowed some samples of paint;
   All shades of the spectrum
   Flowed out of his rectum
With a colourful lack of restraint.

There was a young waiter, called Fritz,
Who got himself fired from The Dorchester,
  When he spilt (what a berk!)
  Chicken soup down the front
Of a lady with rather large hands.

RON RUBIN

The manners of Lady Descartes,
I find more offensive than smart;
    For, whenever I come,
    She lifts up her vast bum,
And emits an earth-shattering fart!

There was a young fellow who started,
Rubbing soap on his arse when it smarted,
    And, to his surprise,
    He received a Grand Prize
For the bubbles he blew when he farted.

Said the Duchess: "Well, yes – I dare say
Toilet paper's all right in its way,
    But, there's nothing so grand
    As some leaves, in one's hand,
When one's out in the woods for the day!"

10.
The Bereft Cleft and Other Tales of Sexual Misfortune

There was a young fellow named Bliss
Whose sex life was strangely amiss;
    For even with Venus
    His recalcitrant penis
Would seldom do better than t
                  h
                  i
                  s

Did you hear about poor Henry Lockett?
He was blown down the street by a rocket;
    The force of the blast
    Blew his balls up his ass,
And his pecker into his top pocket!

A damsel, seductive and handsome,
Got wedged in a sleeping-car transom;
    When she offered much gold
    For release, she was told
That the view was worth more than the ransom!

There was a young lady named Bickers
Whose cousin came off in her knickers;
    But a sperm, at the front,
    Found its way to her cunt,
And they had to pop round to the vicar's.

A pretty young lady named Flo
Said: "I hate to be had in the snow;
    While I'm normally hot,
    In this spot I am not –
So, as soon as you come Joe, let's go!"

There was an old maid from Duluth,
Who wept when she thought of her youth,
  Remembering chances
  She'd missed at school dances,
And once in a telephone booth.

A mortician, who practised in Fyfe,
Made love to the corpse of his wife;
  "I couldn't know, Judge:
  She was cold, didn't budge –
The same as she acted in life!"

"Now really, young man, you're a bore!"
Said Lady Priscilla Flax-Bore,
  "You are covered in sweat,
  And you haven't come yet,
And, my God! it's a quarter past four!"

Another young maid, from New York,
Chose to plug up her cunt with a cork;
  A woodpecker (or yaffle)
  Had a go at that baffle,
But it sure put a stop to the stork!

An ugly old harlot named Gert,
Used to streetwalk until her corns hurt;
  But now she just stands
  Upside down on her hands,
With her face covered up by her skirt.

"With the coffee," Tom said, "I insist
That we each have a large Irish Mist*!"
    But then was unable
    To make it with Mabel,
On account of having
              become
                    alcoholically
                            incapacitated...

CYRIL RAY
*Irish Mist – a sweet, after-dinner liqueur based on Irish whiskey

There was a young lady of Florence,
Who, for kissing, professed an abhorrence;
    But when she'd been kissed
    And found what she'd missed,
She cried till the tears came in torrents.

In Summer, he said, she was fair,
In Autumn, her charms were still there;
    But he said to his wife
    In the Winter of Life:
"There's no Spring in your old derriere!"

I was far from successful with Susie,
A highly imperious floosie,
    Who said; "Try me again,
    But with proper champagne,
Because Susie's too choosy for Bouzy**..."

CYRIL RAY
** A less well-known champagne-producing region

Two middle-aged ladies from Fordham,
Went out for a walk but it bored 'em:
    As they made their way back,
    A crazed sex maniac
Leapt out of a bush and ignored 'em!

She jumped in the car and we sped
To a layby a few miles ahead;
    We came to a stop,
    And she straddled my cock,
But sadly the batteries were dead!

An unfortunate sailor named Bates,
Had performed the fandango on skates;
    But a fall on his cutlass
    Has rendered him nutless
And, well – virtually useless on dates!

There was an old drunkard of Devon,
Who died and ascended to heaven;
  But he cried: "This is Hades –
  There are no naughty ladies,
And the pubs are all shut by eleven!"

RON RUBIN

There was a young fellow named Menzies
Whose kissing sent girls into frenzies;
  But a virgin, one night,
  Crossed her legs in a fright,
And fractured his bi-focal lenzies.

A penniless fellow in Kent,
Had his wife fuck the landlord (lieu: rent);
  But, as she grew older,
  The landlord grew colder,
And now they reside in a tent.

A bashful young fellow of Brighton,
Would never make love with the light on;
  His girlfriend said: "Noel!
  You're in the wrong hole –
There's quite enough room in the right 'un!"

E O PARROTT

There was a young lady of Brabant,
Who slept with an impotent savant;
  She admitted: "We shouldn't,
  But it turned out he couldn't –
So you can't say we have, when we haven't."

All winter a eunuch from Munich,
Went walking in naught but his tunic;
    Folks said: "You'll catch cough,
    And your balls will drop off!"
Said he: "That is why I'm a eunuch."

A nudist, named Roger McPeet,
Loved to dance in the snow and the sleet;
    Till, one chilly December,
    He froze his poor member,
And retired to a monkish retreat.

An accident, really uncanny,
Befell an old lady named Annie:
    She sat on a chair,
    When her false teeth were there,
And bit herself, right on the fanny!

A cook found a poor severed willy
In a pound and a half of Caerphilly;
    She said: "If you please,
    We must not eat this cheese,
But to waste such salami is silly!"

A barrel of lard known as Lyn,
Realized that he'd never be thin;
    He weighed half a ton,
    Not including his bum,
And God knows when he'd last seen his thing!

When drinking a cup of Earl Grey,
My trousers began to decay;
   I clutched at the zip,
   But the old PG Tip
Was determined to have its own way.

An unfortunate lady named Hall,
Wore a newspaper dress to a ball;
   The dress caught on fire
   And burned her entire
Front page, sporting section and all.

A model called Suzy Dunbar,
Committed a dreadful faux pas:
   She loosened a stay
   In her décolleté,
Thus exposing her je ne sais quoi!

There's a sweet chick in Cattahoochee
Who has given my brother VD;
   STDs are a curse,
   Though it might have been worse –
Had I called "heads" it might have been me!"

When Lazarus came back from the dead,
He still couldn't function in bed;
   "What good's Resurrection
   Without an erection?"
Old Lazarus testily said.

Said Fred: "I'd find sex more appealing
If you managed to moan with some feeling."
     Next time he was grafting
     Away at his shafting,
She said: "You've not painted the ceiling!"

"Active balls?" said an old man of Stoneham:
I regret that I no longer own 'em;
     But, I hasten to say,
     They were good in their day –
De mortuis nil nisi bonum.'†

C D CUDMORE

† *Of the dead speak kindly or not at all*

Said Mars when entangled with Venus:
"I feel there is nothing between us,
    And the sound in my ears
    Of Olympian jeers,
Suggests that the blighters have seen us!"

MARY HOLTBY

       There was an old man of Dundee,
       Who came home from the pub, drunkenly;
          He wound up the clock
          With the end of his cock,
       And buggered his wife with the key!

There was an old fellow named Hewing
Whose poor heart stopped while he was screwing;
    He gasped: "Really, miss,
    Don't feel bad about this –
There is nothing I'd rather die doing!"

       A young chap by a girl was desired
       To give her the thrills she required;
          But he died of old age
          Ere his cock could assuage
       The insatiable lusts it inspired!

When the Bermondsey bricklayers struck,
Old Sam Scroggins was 'aving a fuck;
    By union rules
    He 'ad to down tools –
Gor Blimey! What bleedin' 'ard luck!

There was a young princess, Snow White,
Who awoke with a terrible fright;
    She was frightened and shaken –
    She shouldn't have taken
That Seven-Up last thing at night!

GERARD BENSON

An eager young student from Yale,
Was enjoying his first piece of tail;
    He shoved in his pole
    (Whoops! in the wrong hole),
And a voice from beneath yelled: "No sale!"

My back aches, my penis is sore;
I simply can't fuck anymore.
    I'm dripping with sweat,
    And you haven't come yet,
And, my God! it's a quarter past four!

A lady was once heard to weep:
"My poor figure I'm struggling to keep:
    It's my husband's demand
    For a tit in each hand,
And the bugger *will* walk in his sleep!"

There was a young man from Purdue,
Who was only just learning to screw;
    But he hadn't the knack,
    And he got too far back –
In the right church, but in the wrong pew!

The betrothed of an absent crusader,
Entertained every man who waylaid her;
   Till the amorous itch
   Of this popular bitch
So annoyed the crusader he spayed her.

     Ancient octogenarian, Huw,
     To his wife remained steadfastly true;
        This was not from compunction,
        But more the dysfunction
     Of his spermatic glands – nuts to you.

The ageing of man, grumbles Wendy,
Makes it hard to describe him as trendy;
   His joints all go stiff,
   Which would not be bad if
What used to be stiff wasn't bendy!

     Grown tired of her husband's great mass,
     A young bride inserted some glass;
        The prick of her hubby
        Is shorter and stubby,
     While the wife urinates through her ass.

An old couple outside Shrovetide,
Were having great sex, when he died;
   She sat tight on his peak,
   For the rest of the week,
And bounced up and down as she cried.

The King plugged the Queen's ass with mustard
To make her fuck hot, but got flustered:
    He cried: "Oh, my dear,
    I am coming, I fear,
But the mustard will make you come *plus tard!*"

    Said a madam named Mamie La Farge,
    To a sailor ashore from a barge:
        "We have one harlot, dead,
        With a hole in her head,
    But of course there's a small extra charge."

A pretty young maiden named Claire,
Is endowed with a wonderful pair;
    At least, that's what I thought
    Till I saw one get caught
On a thorn and begin losing air!

    Said the whore whom they call Geraldine:
    "When I think of the pricks I have seen,
        And all of the nuts,
        And the assholes and butts,
    And the bastards, like you, in between..."

There was an old curate of Hestion,
Who got hard at the slightest suggestion;
    But, so small was his dick,
    He could scarce screw a tick,
So a tart was quite out of the question.

A quick one-night stand can be hell.
That was what drove Jack back in his shell:
   "It's a bind," he opined,
   "When you find a good grind,
If her husband wants his turn as well!"

JOHN SLIM

Prince Absalom lay with his sister,
And cuddled and nibbled and kissed her;
   But the girl was so tight
   (And it was darkest night),
When he shot at the target – he missed her.

A punter felt rather a prat,
When his todger was trapped and pressed flat;
　　His ardour was damped
　　When he found he was clamped
By a vice girl who really was that!

There was an old Count of Cordoba,
Who would not pay a whore what he owed her;
　So, with great savoir-faire,
　Climbing up on a chair,
She pissed right in his whiskey-and-soda.

There was a young typist named Valerie,
Who had started to count every calorie;
　　Said her boss, in disgust:
　　"If you lose half your bust,
You will only be worth half your salary."

A gallant young Frenchman named Grandhomme,
Tried to copulate riding a tandem;
　At the height of the make,
　She applied the front brake,
And his bollocks were scattered at random.

He approached her with gentle affection
And a pinkly protruding erection;
　　But the love of his life
　　Took a large carving knife
And... (see Diagram 6: Conic Section)

A mini-dinked fellow called Trevor,
Was dismayed when his hardest endeavour
    Produced a wry smile,
    And, after a while:
"Was that it? You don't say! Well, I never!"

      There was a young fellow named Hyde,
      Who took a girl out for a ride;
        He mucked up her fuck-hole,
        And fucked up her muck-hole,
      And charged her five dollars besides.

An anxious young man from Dundee,
Found that after each love-making spree,
    His memory failed,
    And that's why he wailed:
"Who are you, and how was it for me?"

JOHN SLIM

      There was a young girl of Pawtucket,
      Whose box was as big as a bucket;
        Her boyfriend said: "Toots,
        I must wear welly boots,
      For I see I must muck it, not fuck it."

There was a young couple named Kelly,
Who had to live belly to belly;
    Because once, in their haste,
    They'd used wallpaper paste
Instead of petroleum jelly.

Lady C felt her gardener adored her,
(He kept the grounds in such good order);
   But she shot him quite dead:
   There he was, in a bed,
In a pretty, curvaceous young boarder!

DENNIS WALKER

A young Juliet of St Louis,
On a balcony stood, acting screwy;
   Her Romeo climbed,
   But he wasn't well timed,
And halfway up, off he went – blooey!

On the hearthrug in front of the Baxi,
With a filly he'd lured with a fax, he
   Announced: "While I maul you,
   Let me think what to call you."
She replied: "You can call me a taxi!"

In the case of a lady named Frost,
Whose cunt's a good two feet across:
   It's the best part of valour
   To bugger the gal, or
You're apt to fall in and get lost.

An unfortunate joker named Bruce,
Used to greet female friends with a goose,
   Till it came to a stop,
   In a handful of flop,
From some bowels that were terribly loose.

"It's dull in Duluth, Minnesota,
Of spirit there's not an iota,"
  Complained Alice to Joe,
  Who tried hard not to show
That he yawned in her snatch as he blowed her.

Said Susie: "I cannot be thrilled
By a penis whose contents are spilled,
  To leave it diminished
  Before I have finished,
With lots of my lusts unfulfilled."

JOHN SLIM

Said Jane, on the phone to a chum,
Who'd remarked that she sounded quite glum:
   "The trouble is Fred.
   You should see him in bed –
He's lost all his get-up-and-come!"

JOHN SLIM

There was an old lady of Ypres,
Who got shot in the ass by some snipers;
   And when she blew air
   Through her new derriere,
She astounded the Cameron Pipers.

A lady of virginal humours,
Would only be fucked through her bloomers;
   But one fatal day,
   The bloomers gave way,
Which fixed her for future consumers.

There once were two people of taste,
Who were beautiful down to the waist;
   So they limited love
   To those regions above,
And thus remained perfectly chaste.

On their honeymoon, his bride derided
His performance and so he decided
   To buy a vibrator,
   Which he hoped would sate her,
But found batteries were not provided.

There was a young fellow named Rick,
Who was cursed with a spiralling prick;
    So he set out to hunt
    For a screw-twisted cunt
That would match with his corkscrewy dick.

He found one, and took it to bed,
And then, in chagrin, he dropped dead;
    For that spiralling snatch
    Would never quite match –
The damn thing had a left-handed thread!

        There was a young fellow named Charteris,
        Put his hand where his young lady's garter is;
            Said she: "I don't mind,
            But up higher you'll find
        The place where my fucker and farter is!"

There was a young man of Bombay,
Who fashioned a cunt out of clay;
    But the heat of his dick
    Turned it into a brick,
And chafed much of his member away.

        A chap from the Forest of Dean
        Had invented a wanking machine;
            On the ninety-ninth stroke,
            The contraption, whoops, broke
        And converted his bollocks to cream!

A Bavarian dame named Brunhilde,
Went to bed with a jerry-built builder;
   The end of his dong
   Was so poorly put on
That it snapped in her bladder and killed her.

There was an odd fellow named Fletcher,
A lewd and perverted old lecher;
   In a spirit of meanness
   He cut off his penis,
And now he regrets it, I betcha!

A convict despatched to Australia,
Said unto his turnkey: "I'll tail yer!"
   Who said: "You be buggered,
   You filthy old sluggard,
You're forgetting that I am your jailer."

A willing young lady named Grace,
Took as much as she could in her face;
   But a well-endowed lad,
   Giving all that he had,
Blew her tonsils all over the place.

There was a young lady named Sue
Who preferred a stiff drink to a screw;
   One leads to another,
   And now she's a mother –
So, let this be a lesson to you!

Possessive wife, mother of two,
Seeks ugly, withdrawn au pair who
  Won't take time off sick,
  Or tease husband's prick,
Or spend too much time in the loo.

No one can be sure about Myrtle,
As to whether she's sterile or fertile;
  If anyone tries
  To tickle her thighs,
She closes them, tight, like a turtle.

There was a young lady named Rackstraw,
Titallated herself with a hacksaw;
   The result of this action?
   She no longer has traction,
And a penis feels much like a jackstraw.

     There once was a fabulous Creole,
     Whose prick had a wide-open peehole;
       This carrot, so orange,
       Got caught in a door-hinge –
     He'd attempted to bugger the keyhole!

An unfortunate fellow named Puttenham,
Gets his tool caught in doors as he's shuttin 'em;
   Says he: "Yes, perchance,
   It would help to wear pants,
If I'd only remember to button 'em!"

     Floating idly one day through the air,
     A microlight pilot named Blair
       Tied a sizeable rock
       To the end of his cock,
     And fell to earth goodness knows where!

After Chef had got over the shock
Of the mishap involving his cock,
   He elected to serve
   Cock-a-leekie hors d'oeuvres,
Simply adding his knob to the stock.

An efficient young lady named Nance,
Had learned all about fucking in France;
   And when you'd insert it,
   She'd squeeze till she hurt it,
And shove it right back in your pants.

      There was a young fellow named Perkin,
      Who couldn't stop jerking his gherkin;
         His wife said: "Now, Perkin,
         Stop jerking your gherkin –
      You're shirking your ferking, you bastard!"

A horny young fellow named Sledge,
Was jerking off under a hedge;
   The gardener drew near
   With a huge pruning shear,
And trimmed off the edge of his wedge.

      There was a young fellow named Bob,
      Who explained to his friends with a sob:
         "The size of my phallus
         Was perfect for Alice,
      Till she bit off the end of my knob!"

There was a young miss from Torbay,
With an ear, I'm sorry to say,
    Each side of her cleft,
    Which regrettably left
Her lifting one leg, saying: "Eh?"

JOHN SLIM

An unfortunate maiden named Eva,
Was out dancing disguised as Godiva,
    When a change in the lights
    Showed a tear in her tights,
And a big-mouthed young bounder yelled: "Beaver!"

Ninety-seven last Tuesday, old Wynn
Is still visiting brothels, to sin;
    With a triumphant shout,
    He will get his cock out,
But it's so limp he can't get it in!

There was a young fellow named Bryn,
Whose prick was so small and so thin,
    His wife found she needed
    A telescope (she did),
To see if he'd gotten it in.

To his bride a young bridegroom said: "Pish!
But your cunt is as big as a dish!"
    She replied: "Why, you fool,
    With your limp little tool,
It's like driving a nail with a fish!"

There was a young fellow called Bright,
Who never got form-filling right;
    When the question was: Sex?
    Without further checks,
He wrote down: "On Saturday night".

JOHN SLIM

You'll have heard that knock-kneed Sammy Wuzzum,
Wed Samantha, his bow-legged cousin?
   Though observers will say
   Love will find its own way,
Not for Sam and Samantha it doesn'.

A sassy young lassie named Jacquelyn,
Was classed as a crass piece of cracquelyn;
    Her slot was so slight
    That, try as they might,
The lads couldn't quite get their tacquelyn.

JOHN SLIM

There was a young girl named McCall,
Whose pussy was, well – fairly small;
   But the size of her anus
   Was something quite heinous!
It could hold seven members in all.

There was a young girl from Pitlochry,
Who was had by a cad in the rockery;
    Said she: "Oh, you've come
    All over my bum –
This isn't a fuck, it's a mockery!"

Galapagos Gough was a toff
Who amused himself jacking it off;
   He tugged it so hard
   It stretched almost a yard,
Turned a brilliant blue, and fell off!

      A limp alcoholic named Hughes,
      Who's promised to give up the booze,
         Admits: "When I'm muddled,
         My senses get fuddled,
      And I miss out on too many screws."

There was a young fellow of Rhodes,
Whose poor testicles turned into toads;
   As they lolloped and leapt,
   He, quite horrified, wept:
"Give me back my quiescent old nodes!"

      There was a young fellow from Lees,
      Who handled his tool with great ease;
         The continual friction
         Made his member a fiction –
      But the callus hangs down to his knees.

A fellow whose cock catches fire,
Whenever he burns with desire,
   Has found that this means
   He singes his jeans
While watching the Luton Girls' Choir.

JOHN SLIM

A nervous young girl from New York,
Is so cautious, from fear of the stork,
   To prevent being raped,
   You'll find she is duct-taped,
And her asshole is plugged with a cork!

So I guess that's a 'NO'

There was an old spinster named Mair,
Who shouted: "My pussy's on fire!"
   The firemen (when found)
   Brought their engine around,
And extinguished her burning desire.

Remember those two from Aberystwyth,
Who connected the things that they pissed with?
    She sat on his lap,
    But they both had the clap,
And they cursed with the things that they kissed with.

        There was a young bounder named Snyder,
        Who dated a girl just to ride her;
            She allowed him to feel
            From her neck to her heel,
        But she wouldn't permit him inside her.

There was an old goddess named Venus,
Who adored young Adonis' penis;
    When Jupiter (fool!)
    Cut off the boy's tool,
She remarked: "Please do not come between us."

        To the city went sweet Dolly Dare,
        Quite determined to have an affair;
            But her wishes miscarried –
            The guys were all married;
        Still, I'll bet she played no solitaire!

A widow whose singular vice
Was to keep her late husband on ice,
    Said: "It's hard since I lost him –
    I'll never defrost him!
Cold comfort, but cheap at the price."

An unlucky old duffer named Mort,
Owned a penis so miserably short,
   That his lady friend said,
   As he clambered in bed:
"I suppose it's a cock – of a sort!"

There's a keen working-girl named Hortense,
Who will charge you a meagre ten cents;
   When a fella won't pay,
   She will play anyway,
Though it does make poor Hortense the whore tense.

This poor little chap's such a dork!
He thinks he's been brought by the stork;
   But his dad's not much better:
   He bought a french letter,
And tested its strength with a fork!

An incompetent fellow named Fred
Took a confident maiden to bed;
   When he'd diddled a while,
   She observed with a smile:
"Well, you've got it all in, but the head."

There's a feckless young fellow named Goody
Who insists that he wouldn't, but would he?
   If he finds himself nude,
   With girls in the right mood,
The question's not would he, but could he?

The tiniest penis I've seen
Was no bigger than this, but quite clean –
   It had shrunk such a lot
   On a setting (too hot)
In a spinner-rinse washing machine!

      A young chap whose sight was myopic,
      Believed sex such an interesting topic;
         Though so poor were his eyes,
         That, despite its great size,
      His appendage appeared microscopic.

There was a prick-teaser named Jeanie,
Whose boyfriends thought she was a meanie;
   Out necking at night,
   She would close her legs tight,
And do little but play with your weenie.

      A remorseful, old lecher named Poole,
      Soliloquized thus to his tool:
         "From Cape Cod to Salamanca,
         You've had pox, clap and chancre –
      Now ain't you the world's biggest fool!"

A quite keen but still virginal Celt,
Had an urge to know how a cock felt;
   One went in, hard and straight,
   But the heat was so great,
She unwittingly caused it to melt!

There was an old spinster named Campbells,
Who got hopelessly tangled in brambles;
   Cried she: "Ouch! It sticks,
   Though so many sharp pricks
Aren't encountered that often on rambles."

There was an old duffer named Skinner,
Whose prick, his wife said, had grown thinner;
   But still, by and large,
   It would always discharge –
That is – once he could get the thing in her!

An insatiable bounder named Fletcher,
Was renowned as a tireless lecher;
   When he mounted a whore,
   She would need a rebore,
And they'd carry him out on a stretcher!

An overweight man from Rangoon,
Had a prick not unlike a balloon;
   When he got it inside her,
   And started to ride her,
She thought she was pregnant too soon.

A beautiful maiden named Psyche,
Is adored by a fellow named Mikey;
   One thing about Mike
   The poor girl cannot like
Is his prick, which is awfully spikey.

When he'd died his wife cried as if
Heartbroken, but then with a sniff
  Sobbed: "Fifty years wed
  And now that he's dead
The bastard has learnt to stay stiff."

NICK TOCZEK

Ex-telephonist Gladys, I'm told
(Now a tart with a heart of pure gold),
  Sympathizes with tricks
  Minus lead in their dicks,
And quite happily puts them on hold.

There was an old man who said: "Tush!
My balls always hang in the brush,
    And I fumble about,
    Halfway in and half out,
With a pecker as limber as mush."

       There was a young fellow named Murray,
       Making love to his girl in a surrey;
          As she started to sigh,
          Somebody happened by,
       So he buttoned his pants in a hurry.

A lusty young woodsman of Maine,
Who for years with no woman had lain;
    Found some sublimation,
    At a high elevation,
In the cleft of a pine – God, the pain!

       Oedipus Oedipus Oedipus Smith
       Could copulate only with kin and/or kith;
          Till they cut off his penis,
          Whence thereafter Venus
       To him was a quite unattainable myth.

There was a young girl named Dalrymple,
Whose genital parts were so simple:
    On looking, they found
    Little more than a mound,
In the middle of which was a pimple!

An unhappy girl named Hillfiger,
Cried aloud as she squeezed on the trigger:
    "You son-of-a-bitch!
    My cunt has the itch,
And in *morte* you may attain *rigor*."

        An old doctor who lacked protoplasm,
        Tried to give his young wife an orgasm;
            But his tongue jumped the track
            'Twixt the front and the back,
        And got caught in a bad anal spasm.

There was a young girl whose frigidity,
Approached cataleptic rigidity;
    Till you gave her a drink,
    When she quickly would sink
In a state of complaisant liquidity.

        Determined she'd not be disgraced,
        Young Diane fled all suitors in haste;
            And it all went so well,
            Till she stumbled and fell –
        She still sometimes imagines she's chaste.

There was a young man from the coast,
Who had an affair with a ghost;
    Said the pallid phantasm
    At the height of orgasm,
"I think I can feel it – almost!"

There was a young Georgian named Lynd,
Who had never, in all his life, sinned;
 For, whenever he'd start,
 He'd be jarred by a fart,
And his semen was gone with the wind.

A newly-wed couple called Birch,
Were driving away from the church;
 Said the bride: "I could go for
 That hunky young chauffeur!"
And left her poor spouse in the lurch.

RON RUBIN

There was an old spinster named Gretel,
Who wore underclothes made of metal;
 When they asked: "Does it hurt?"
 She replied: "It keeps dirt
From stamen and pistil and petal."

There was a young lady of Harwich,
Who pronounced on the morn of her marriage:
 "I shall sew my chemise
 All the way to my knees –
I am damned if I'll fuck in the carriage!"

A m-milkmaid there was, with a s-stutter,
Who was lonely and longed for a f-futter;
    She had n-nowhere to t-turn,
    So she d-diddled a ch-churn,
And m-m-managed to come with the b-butter.

A clever old eunuch of Roylem,
Took two eggs to the cook and said: "Boil 'em.
    I'll hang them beneath
    My inadequeate sheath,
    And slip into the harem, and foil 'em!"

The physicians of Baroness Trapp,
Found a terrible rash on her map –
    Sores that opened and closed,
    Which they soon diagnosed
As a case of perennial clap.

There was a young lady of Michigan,
Who said: "Blast it! I'm getting the itch again."
    Said her mother: "That's strange,
    I'm surprised it ain't mange,
    If you've slept with that son-of-a-bitch again!"

A widow who lived in Rangoon,
Placed a black-ribboned wreath on her womb;
    "To remind me," she said
    "Of my husband, who's dead,
And of what put him into his tomb."

A keen, unfulfilled lady from Brent,
Whose old hubby's poor pecker had bent,
    Remarked, with a sigh:
    "Why, oh, why must it die?"
And injected some Portland Cement!

        A bashful young lady of India,
        Asked the Colonel: "Is fucking a sin, dear?"
            In a voice slurred with gin,
            He replied: "It's a sin
        When I can't get the fucking thing in, dear!"

        RON RUBIN

A finicky young whippersnapper,
Has a habit annoyingly dapper;
    So, no willing girl's quim
    Ever interests him,
If it hasn't a cellophane wrapper!

        An award-winning chemist from Utah
        Is devising a condom of pewter;
            He admits: "I confess
            To feel nothing, or less,
        But it makes one as safe as a neuter!"

Despite all the poking and prising,
My cock ain't about to start rising;
    It's not that it's colder,
    I'm just getting older,
And you'll have to get used to down-sizing!

A king sadly said to his queen:
"In parts you have grown far from lean."
   "I don't give a damn,
   You've always liked ham,"
She replied, and he gasped: "How obscene!"

When a fat striptease dancer debuted
At an Old Boys' Reunion in Buted,
   Cried a diner: "By gum –
   What a hideous bum!
You're putting me right off my futed!"

RON RUBIN

A misguided harlot, a new kid,
Has done something incredibly stupid:
   When her lover had spent,
   She douched with cement,
And gave birth to a statue of Cupid.

       There was a young lady from China,
       Who confused her mouth with her vagina;
          Her clitoris (huge)
          She covered with rouge,
       And lipsticked her labia minor.

A chap, who hails from Oklahoma,
Had a cock that could sing La Paloma;
   But the sweetness of pitch
   Couldn't outweigh the hitch
Of his impotence, size and aroma.

       There was a young bridegroom of Strensall,
       Whose prick was as sharp as a pencil;
          The night of his wedding,
          It tore through the bedding,
       And shattered the chamber utensil.

An unfortunate fellow named Paul,
Has admitted he's only one ball,
   But the size of his prick
   Is God's dirtiest trick,
For the girls always ask: "Is that all?"

A victim of sexual repression
Went through a sex therapy session;
    But more efficacious
    Was a lovely, curvaceous
Young girl of the oldest profession.

RON RUBIN

A new bride was heard, sadly, to say:
"Goodness me, I am wearing away!
    The insides of my thighs
    Are akin to mince pies –
For my husband won't shave every day!"

Consider the Emperor Nero –
Of many lewd tales he's the hero;
    Though he scraped on the fiddle,
    He just couldn't diddle –
And his true batting average was zero.

An elderly lady of Arden,
Whose gamekeeper's tool wouldn't harden,
    Declared, with a frown,
    "I've been sadly let down
By the tool of a fool in the garden."

A generous lady named Beaulieu,
Has often been screwed by yours truly;
    But, by now – it's appalling –
    My balls always fall in,
For I fear I have fucked her unduly.

"How much," sighed the gentle Narcissus,
"A man of my character misses!
  It is clear, on reflection,
  I've got an erection,
But all I can do is blow kisses."

STEPHEN SYLVESTER

When he tried to insert his huge whanger,
A young airman aroused his girl's anger;
  As they groped in the dark,
  She was heard to remark:
"What you need is an aeroplane hangar!"

An unfulfilled caterer, Kate,
Often questioned her virginal state:
    Why did men pay to meet
    Such crude whores on the street,
When they could have had *her* on a plate!

A desperate old harpy from Umsk,
Who was sadly unable to cumsk,
    Would ecstatically shout
    When a samovar spout
Was shoved up her Muscovite rumpsk.

KEITH SHEPHERD

She's naked in bed with a wimp
Whose little pink prick's like a shrimp;
    They'd screw if it grew stiff,
    But he's much too skew-whiff
On lager, and that's why it's limp!

NICK TOCZEK

A frigid young lady from Gloucester,
Once had an affair on the coucester;
    "She's cold as gazpacho,"
    Complained her muchacho,
"But I'm doing my best to defroucester!"

RON RUBIN

The sex claims of most men disguise
The fact that they boast and tell lies;
    If we called them wankers,
    I doubt that they'd thank us –
Though few screw, while more come handwise.

NICK TOCZEK

Well, you may be a famous MP,
But you're not all you're cracked up to be;
    I just can't remember
    When your standing member
Last lost its deposit in me!

There was a young lady of Kent,
Who said that she knew what it meant
　　When men asked her to dine,
　　Gave her cocktails and wine,
She knew what it meant – but she went.

Not that it always transpired
That it turned out the way she desired:
　　One gent from Kent
　　Was undoubtedly bent
And he didn't advance – he retired . . .

CYRIL RAY

WHERE TO DO IT

Hall, kitchen table, landing, loo,
Garage, garden, gazebo, zoo,
　　Car (but park it),
　　Supermarket,
Graveyard, cinema, barbecue.

Back of a taxi, in the Med,
Roof top, chip shop, hospital bed,
　　Skiing, boating,
　　While you're voting,
Seashore, bookstore, bicycle shed.

Bus, bath, balcony, best friend's flat,
Larder, library, laundromat.
　　Lay-by, bi-plane,
　　Bed, shed, tube train,
Hot-tub, haunted habitat.

Cave mouth, caravan, country seat,
Doorway, dining room, darkened street,
　　Shelter, shower,
　　Tudor tower,
Hotel, motel, honeymoon suite.

Stadium, staircase, works canteen,
Pub, pavilion, submarine,
　　Boardroom, bandstand,
　　Workplace, wasteland,
Washroom, penthouse, loft, limousine.

Your place, my place, alleyway, squat,
Battlements, basement, sofa, cot,
　　Dungeon, diner,
　　Ocean liner,
If you're celibate, maybe not.

NICK TOCZEK

A young woman, from Berwick-on-Tweed,
Although comely, was very knock-kneed;
　Her boyfriend called Andy,
　However, was bandy –
'Twas amusing to watch them proceed!

IAN HERBERT

His bride said: "We'll fuck in the dark,
On our honeymoon night, near the park."
　　His manhood thus slighted,
　　He thought: "Right!" and invited
His identical twin, for a lark.

"THE LAST RIDE TOGETHER"
(With apologies to Robert Browning)

"Is it thou?" "Ay!" cried Fra Lippo Lippi,
"'Zooks, lass, 'tis confoundedly nippy.
　　But slip out of your gown
　　And I'll give you a crown
Or two more, but we'd best make it slippy."

So they up and went at it like knives,
Or they humped (shall I say?) 'sthough their lives
　　Were dependent on what
　　They performed; and they got
To the climax in just twenty drives

Of the loins. She sighed: "Flower of the vine,
My God! You are perfectly mine;
　　'Tis enough. Keep your gold.
　　But my love, I grow cold.
Where's 'e gone? Where's my gown? Br-r-r you swine!"

JEDEDIAH BARROW

A wealthy old man from Niagara,
Whose car-sex was fuelled by Viagra,
　　Was parked near The Falls,
　　When his prick 'n' balls
Got ate by his tool-eater Jaguar.

NICK TOCZEK

There was a young fellow named Fyffe,
Whose marriage was ruined for life;
   He had an aversion
   To every perversion,
And only liked fucking his wife.

Well, one year the poor woman struck,
And she wept, as she cursed her bad luck;
   Wailing: "Where has it gotten us –
   You're goddamn monotonous
F-f-fuck after fuck after fuck?"

Marital fidelity is a weird perversion

Let me tell you the think that I've thunk –
If you're drinking too much you'll be drunk:
   So whilst you are drinking
   Try not to get stinking,
For if stinking you'll stink like a skunk.

And be warned by the wink that I've wunk –
No need to be meek as a monk,
   But I trust you'll be able
   To rise from the table
And find your way home to your bunk.

For this is the fear that I funk –
That if in a stupor you're sunk,
   You'll be buzzed by the fuzz,
   In the way the fuzz does,
And that then into clink you'll be clunk...

CYRIL RAY

Said the Marquis de Sade: "I'm inventive,
When my lovers become inattentive:
   Without pain there's no gain
   I explain with my cane
To achieve an erotic incentive."

JANET SMITH

There was a young lady from Ware
Who had an astonishing pair:
    One, listing to port,
    Was the usual sort,
But the starboard side tit was quite square!

KEITH SHEPHERD

A lad of the brainier kind
Had erogenous zones in his mind;
    He liked the sensations
    Of solving equations
So much, in the end he went blind!

Here he comes, little cocky Cock Robin,
Bob bob bob bob bob bob bob a-bobbin;
   But look! Two great tits
   Are attacking his bits,
And will leave his poor sore cock a-throbbin!

An unfaithful old bounder, called Reg,
Had neglected his marital pledge,
   Till his long-suffering wife
   Fetched her best kitchen knife
And removed (ouch!) his meat and two veg!

"Oh, halt!" cried Virginia, "Enough!
It's not that your beard is too rough;
   Indeed it's benign
   So close up to mine,
But why not attempt the real stuff?"

OTTO WATTEAU

I went straight round but to no avail,
Though the advert said: Large Chest For Sale,
   And mentioned deep drawers –
   I thought: "Pray, show me yours."
But she sold me an old Chippendale.

In the Sex Shop, Fiona's heart sank,
But she'd only herself she could thank;
   She enthused: "I'll have that!"
   The assistant said: "Drat –
That one's mine, I was having a wank!"

A young scuba-diver, Persemony,
Encountered a monstrous anemone;
   Deep under the sea
   It seized her with glee,
And gobbled her *pudenda feminae*!

The first time I met Gypsy Rose,
In what seemed a provocative pose,
   I realized she
   Wasn't Gypsy Rose Lee –
And I asked her to replace her clothes.

Take the case of the Duchess Lacoste
Whose pudenda are three feet across:
   It's the best part of valour
   To bugger the gal, or
One's inclined to fall in, and get lost!

There once was a newspaper vendor,
A person of dubious gender;
   He'd agree, if you'd queue,
   To allow you to view
His remarkable cockeyed pudenda.

There was a young fellow, from Florida,
Who liked a friend's wife, so he borrowed her;
   When they jumped into bed,
   He cried: "God! Strike me dead!
This isn't a cunt – it's a corridor!"

There once was a sensitive bride,
Who ran when the groom she'd espied;
    She had spotted the size
    Of the thing twixt his thighs –
When he caught her, and fucked her, she sighed . . .

I was sitting there, taking my ease,
And enjoying my Beaumes-de-Venise,
    With a charming young poppet,
    But she told me to stop it
As my fingers crept up past her knees.

CYRIL RAY

The one-bollocked spouse of our Kitty,
Is deserving of anyone's pity;
　　Except that the catch is
　　His deficiency matches
Our Kitty, who has but one titty!

A squeamish young fellow named Bland,
Thought caressing his penis was grand;
　　But he viewed, with distaste,
　　The gelatinous paste
That it left in the palm of his hand.

Though fellows have frequently found
That testicles don't make a sound,
　　With a lad in Seattle,
　　They're metal, and rattle,
And probably weigh several pound!

An un-endowed stripper, named Ron,
Did charity shows in Saigon;
　　They'd always complain:
　　"Oh, not him again!"
And they cheered when he put things back on.

JOHN SLIM

There was a young fellow from Yale,
Whose face was exceedingly pale;
   He'd spent his vacation
   In self-masturbation,
Because of the high price of tail.

      When Molly met Milly in Walmart,
      She really did not look at all smart:
         Her blouse lacked a press,
         And it's anyone's guess
      Why she wears such short skirts for a tall tart!

Said a goose-pimpled stripper of Preston:
"It's the coldest night that I've undressed on.
   D'you think folk will mind
   If I bare my behind
Whilst sensibly keeping my vest on?"

      The big toe of a postman in Dallas,
      Had developed a sizeable callus;
         His wife (wistfully) said
         How she wished that, instead,
      It had been on the head of his phallus.

A young trapeze artiste named Bracht,
Is faced with a very sad fact:
    Imagine his pain
    When, again and again,
He catches his wife in the act!

        A myopic young fellow named Clark,
        Raped a Giant Redwood, in the dark;
            What a splendid surprise!
            Oh, such tightness and size!
        But his poor knob was scraped by the bark.

A practical joker, named Ron,
Strapped a pair of huge false knockers on,
    Then got pissed at a party,
    And acted so tarty
That things soon began to go wrong . . .

        There was a young lady of Lydd,
        Who'd stuttered since being a kid;
            When asked for a lay,
            Before she could say:
        She d-d-d-didn't, she did!

All those years he'd ignored her pudenda –
For all he cared she was non-gender;
    Then one night, out of spite,
    She thought: "I'll put him right!"
And she puréed his cock in the blender.

A languid young fellow, from Goole,
Lightly touched (with the tip of his tool)
   A high-voltage wire;
   Though his pubes then caught fire,
He retained what remained of his cool.

A stripper who stripped in Ceylon,
Suspected her best days had gone,
   When she finished her act,
   And was faced with the fact
That the customers roared: "Gerremon!"

A po-faced young stripper, from Fairlie,
Who smiled, if at all, fairly rarely,
   Was asked, by some berk,
   How she fancied her work –
She gritted her teeth and said: "Barely!"

JOHN SLIM

Said a lonely old man called Le Mesurier:
"If I had a girlfriend, I'd treasurier!"
   Well, he found a cute filly,
   But by that time his willy
Was wholly unable to pleasurier.

RON RUBIN

A slow-screwing fellow, from Ayr,
Caused Clare, who was there, to declare:
   "If you're not in full flow
   In a minute, just go."
But he came with six seconds to spare!

JOHN SLIM

She exclaimed, while replacing the truss
Of a gruesome old geezer named Gus:
   "If you were a gent,
   You'd have said what you meant,
When you told me you'd come on the bus!"

If you have a hard-on, she'll clock it,
Asking: "Is that a gun in your pocket?"
   Though it's true that Miss West
   May be well past her best,
Still a fuck is a fuck – so don't knock it.

There was an old fellow called Frank,
Whose penis quite suddenly shrank;
   Although it looked cute,
   It was far too minute
To provide an acceptable wank.

RON RUBIN

To the whore, said the cold Lady Fizzit:
"The Lord's a new man since your visit;
　　As a rule, the old fool
　　Can't erect his damned tool!
You must have what it takes, but what is it?"

"Supposing I bonk with my brother,"
Said Sue, "Though a bit of the other –
　　Don't worry, I shan't –
　　It would make me the aunt
Of a baby to which I was mother!"

JOHN SLIM

Old Geoffrey and Flo, who was flirty,
Had sneaked off to bed at six-thirty,
   Where Flo, who was deaf,
   Insisted to Geoff:
"Whatever else happens, shout dirty!"

      Nymphomaniac, dainty Eleanor,
      Finds that most male organs now pain her;
         "It seems I have blundered,"
         She says, "Seven hundred?
      Far too many for one small container!"

Dear doctor, I need your advice:
When excited my cock shoots Old Spice!
   I make love quite poorly,
   And come prematurely –
But the girls always say they smell nice!

      There was a young lady, named Glad,
      Whose stutter was ever so bad;
         Because of her stutter,
         By the time she could utter
      She w-w-w-wouldn't, she had!

A train-spotting couple of Harwich,
Took time off to celebrate marriage;
   Its brief consummation
   Took place at Crewe Station
In the back of an old railway carriage.

RON RUBIN

Said an anxious young fellow in Goring:
"Could it be that you think I am boring?
 It's throbbing. I'm bobbing.
 You're getting a knobbing,
But you're so sound asleep that you're snoring!"

JOHN SLIM

A gentleman said: "When I doff
My hat to a lady I cough;
 "Ahem!" I will say,
 "What a beautiful day!"
The lady may then say: "Piss off!"

There was a young virgin named Jeanie,
Whose dad was an absolute meanie;
 When he'd fashioned a hatch,
 With a latch, for her snatch –
She could only be had by Houdini!

Pray tell me, dear, who is that chump
Who stands there, all naked and plump,
 With his tool in his ear,
 Appearing, from here,
Like a rather obscene petrol pump?

Though Pat's tied the knot with young Pete,
Their happiness isn't complete;
 He hasn't been right
 Since their honeymoon night,
Which they spent in the Nutcracker Suite!

Her fiancé, a bit of a toff,
Had morals which caused her to scoff;
   "I'll not use it," he said,
   "Not until we are wed!"
And that's why she's broken it off.

JOHN SLIM

      There was a young lady, named Marge,
      Whose boobs were abnormally large;
         She'd trap all your fingers
         Between her great swingers,
      Then smile, and insist: "There's no charge!"

      JOHN SLIM

Moaned a mountainous couple, bereft:
"Because of our size we are left
   With a see-saw arrangement
   Of navel engagement,
Which tends to exclude cock and cleft!"

JOHN SLIM

      She yelled at her husband: "You prat!"
      When he died on the job at their flat;
         But she soon grew inured
         To the loss she'd endured –
      Rigor mortis was seeing to that!

At sex he was never adept,
On Viagra, erect but inept;
   Though he did make amends
   For his wife and her friends
Who queued up for quoits while he slept!

JOHN SLIM

An eager inventor, named Jones,
Was reduced to loud sobbing and moans;
   He'd devised X-ray glasses
   To study clothed lasses,
But all he could see were their bones!

When a feminine itch made her ill,
She consulted the doctor: "A pill?"
   But the Doc's diagnosis
   Was pediculosis –
He advised her to call Rentokil!

JANET SMITH

       There was a short-kilted North Briton
       Who, for kinkiness, sat on a kitten;
          But the pussy had claws –
          The immediate cause
       Of the somewhat abrupt circumcision.

Newly wed to a wanker, the bride
Watched his first-night performance and sighed;
   Then, still deep in shock,
   Left a note on his cock:
"My cleft is bereft. Come inside!"

JOHN SLIM

       Said a voice from the back of the car:
       "Young man, I don't know who you are,
          But allow me to state,
          Though it may be too late:
       I had not meant to come quite this far!"

There's a fellow whose cocktail quips
Fail to charm any chick as she sips;
   Between sips, her lips say:
   "You're a bore – go away!"
Between sighs, her eyes say: "Read my lips!"

A precocious young lady named Hall,
Once attended a birth-control ball;
   She was loaded with pessaries,
   And other accessories –
But no one approached her at all!

Breaking off from a kiss, with delight,
Fred declared: "You're a bit of all right!
   What a smacker! Oh, brother!
   D'you fancy another?"
She said: "Yes, but he's busy tonight!"

JOHN SLIM

There was a young lady called Ransom,
Who was serviced four times in a Hansom;
   When she cried: "Give me more!"
   A weak voice from the floor
Protested: "It's Simpson, not Samson!"

I heard of a story so fraught
With disaster, of balls that got caught,
   When a chap took a crap
   In the woods, and a trap
Underneath . . . oh, I can't bear the thought!

It seemed all was well for old Bill;
The night was romantic and still:
   She was warm, she was waiting,
   She was ripe for the mating,
But alas – she was not on the pill!

      Said the newlyweds staying near Kitely:
      "We turn out the electric light nightly;
         It's best to embark
         Upon sex in the dark –
      The look of the thing's so unsightly!"

Don't ever dare do that again!
If you're tempted to, kindly refrain!
   People pointed and spluttered,
   And stood back and muttered,
And then wanted me to explain!

      There was a young fellow from Kent,
      Whose tool was incredibly bent;
         To save himself trouble,
         He put it in double,
      And, instead of coming, he went!

There was a young lawyer named Rex,
Who was sadly deficient in sex:
    Arraigned for exposure
    He said, with composure:
"*De minimis non curat lex!*"**

***The Law is not concerned with trifles.*

        A naked young temptress called Kitty,
        Reclines on the beach (very pretty):
            But "No, stop!" she blurts,
            "Pull it out quick, it hurts –
        It's all covered in sand and it's gritty!"

A sprightly old codger from Goring,
Was asked why he'd taken up whoring;
    "Straightforward," he said,
    "My wife is stone-dead,
And necrophilia's simply dead boring!"

        At a hundred, my Great Uncle Ned
        Took a sexy young slapper to bed;
            I'm afraid I can't say
            If he had it away,
        'Cos it's wrong to speak ill of the dead!

She cried: "You're a filthy old fart!"
While he practised his lecherous art;
    "Why here? Why me?
    Why Central Dundee?
And why in a roadsweeper's cart?"

How bitter was Joseph's existence
When he found that his girlfriend's insistence
   Meant that he'd have to wed her
   Before he could bed her –
She was simply a pièce de résistance!

ISAAC ASIMOV

There was a young welder from Reading,
Who was constantly wetting the bedding,
   Till his mother, one day,
   In a wearisome way,
Suggested a girl, and a wedding.

   A computer buff's ancient jalopy
   Is where the young ladies get stroppy:
      Though they strive to survive
      Without a hard drive,
   Very few can make do on a floppy!

There was a Countess from the Chase,
Who was woefully lacking in grace;
   In the midst of a kiss,
   She started to piss,
Which was neither the time, nor the place.

Those bedsprings! The twang and the creaks
Have kept me awake for two weeks;
    Why do newly-weds
    Always use squeaky beds
To practise their screwing techniques?

    Their friends are all deeply upset
    With a sadness they'll never forget;
        Jack and Jill, it appears,
        Were happy for years –
    Then fate took a hand, and they met!

JOHN SLIM

The couple upstairs are from Ealing;
They're insatiable I've a strong feeling:
    They scream when they're grinding,
    And, of late, I've been finding
A network of cracks in my ceiling!

        When Oedipus plunged in, erect,
        Jocasta cried: "Cease! I object –
            You're a Greek, screw some other –
            Your friend, or your brother –
        Mother-fucking is somewhat suspect!"

Said a man from Mobile, Alabama:
"I'm displeased with my role in life's drama!
    My wife, who's a shrew,
    Isn't willing to screw,
And she's sure to outlive me, God damn her!"

ISAAC ASIMOV

        A spotty young schoolboy named Ned
        Used to masturbate nightly in bed;
            Said his mother: "Dear lad,
            That's exceedingly bad –
        Why not jump in with Mama instead?"

Old Harold declared: "I maintain
A condom's not safe. I'll explain:
   I wore one today
   And, I'm sorry to say,
I got myself hit by a train!"

JOHN SLIM

A sultan said sadly: "One strives
To please all of my fifty-six wives,
   But, alas, intromission
   Gives me the condition
That's commonly known as 'the hives'."

ISAAC ASIMOV

The frigid Viscountess of Gloucester,
Hired a gigolo, named Fancy Foster;
    She was poked, by this pro,
    Seven times in a row –
It took the first six to defrost her!

At death's door lay old Lady Phipps,
(No man had yet mounted her hips);
    So the postillion tried her –
    By heck! Did he ride her!
And she died with a smile on her lips.

There was an old strumpet, from Cheadle,
Who imparted the clap to the beadle;
    When she asked: "Does it itch?"
    He replied: "Yes, you bitch –
And it burns like hellfire when I peedle!"

A woman from South Philadelphia,
Once found herself left on the shelphia;
    No one wanted her wares,
    But she muttered: "Who cares?"
And cheerfully played with herselphia.

ISAAC ASIMOV

The bride first turned pink, then bright red:
"I couldn't touch that thing!" she said;
   But now she's all right,
   Having practised all night
In the dark, with a sausage, in bed.

JOHN SLIM

A frustrated virgin, young Joan,
Told her boyfriend one midnight in Rome:
   If that willy stays dead,
   You can hop out of bed,
Get your togs on, and bugger off home!

A policewoman got quite a buzz
From a plain-clothes patrol just because
   Her cover was blown
   When a crook, who'd not known,
Did a full-frontal grope and yelled "Fuzz!"

JOHN SLIM

A forgetful young man of Capri,
Is resigned to a mind all at sea;
   Throughout married life,
   He's been asking his wife:
"Who are you? And how was it for me?"

JOHN SLIM

There was a young fellow from Purley,
Who'd never fulfilled any girlie;
   His minimal dick
   Used to come so damn quick –
It was always too little, too early.

JOHN SLIM

A beau, who for years had been hunted
By girls, found his charms had been blunted
   By food he'd encased,
   Which had all gone to waist,
And finally made him beau-fronted!

JOHN SLIM

A sex-bomb whose figure's fantastic
Has altered her shape something drastic:
   She's not looked the same
   Since her dad's Zimmer-frame
Got stuck in her knicker elastic!

JOHN SLIM

The doctor's cock's quite hard to see,
And poor Igor's appendage is wee;
   When all's said and done,
   I like chaps well-hung –
So, it's Frankenstein's Monster for me!

A women who lived in St Paul,
Had breasts undeniably small;
    Her husband growled: "Dear,
    Why not burn your brassière?
It's fulfilling no function at all!"

ISAAC ASIMOV

I never have thoughts of another
Whilst wrapped in the arms of my lover,
    Though her overall size,
    And those great hairy thighs
Often put me in mind of my brother!

A hapless young fellow named Shmuck,
Considers himself out of luck;
    Though he's petted and wooed,
    When he tries to get screwed,
He finds virgins just don't give a fuck.

Another young lady named Hopper,
Has become a society cropper;
    She determined to go
    To Bordeaux with her beaux –
But the rest of the story's improper.

11.
The Dark Deeds of the Dean of Westminster and Other Irreverent Limericks

An old preacher from Idaho Springs,
Always talked about God and such things;
   But his secret desire
   Was a guy in the choir,
With a bottom like jelly on springs!

The Dean undressed, with heaving breast,
The Bishop's wife to lie on;
   He thought it lewd
   To do it nude,
So, he kept his old school tie on!

A churchman, austere and refined,
Caught with hand gripping lady's behind,
   Cried: "Our ministry's such
   That we must keep in touch
With the widely felt needs of mankind!"

There was a fair lady from Bangor,
Who drove young men frantic with anger,
   By going to matins
   In see-through white satins,
Till the vicar was forced to harangue her.

There was an old Abbess, quite shocked,
To find nuns where the candles were locked;
   Said the Abbess: "You nuns
   Should behave more like guns –
And never go off till you're cocked!"

When a horny old curate in Leeds,
Was discovered one day in the weeds
   Astride a young nun,
   He cried; "God! This is fun!
So much better than telling one's beads!"

     Of Ufford there was an old Rector,
     Who served as the choirboy inspector;
        He blessed them in pairs,
        And concluded affairs
     With two thrusts of his rectal injector.

     GORDON THORBURN

The Reverend Mr Uprightly,
Was cuckolded both daily and nightly;
   He murmured: "Oh, dear!
   I would fain interfere,
If I knew how to do it politely."

     There was a young lady named Smith,
     Whose virtue was largely a myth;
        She said: "Try as I can,
        I cannot find a man
     Who it's fun to be virtuous with!"

There was a young lady called Lynne,
Who was deep in original sin;
   When they said; "Do be good!"
   She said: "Would if I could!"
And went, straightaway, at it again!

An amorous lassie, named Harriet,
Took on two willing lads in a chariot,
   Then – six monks and four tailors,
   Nine priests, seven sailors,
Mohammed and Judas Escariot!

There was a young maiden of Chichester,
Who made all the saints in their niches stir;
   One morning, at matins,
   Her breasts in white satins
Made the Bishop of Chichester's breeches stir!

There once was a monk, of Camyre,
Who was seized with a carnal desire;
   And the primary cause
   Were the Abbesses' drawers
Which were hanging to dry by the fire!

An insatiable Anglican pastor
Whose old cleaner let little slip past her,
   Said: "If you must go for
   Your sex on the sofa,
Please ensure there's an antimacassar!"

There was an old bounder named Baker,
Who seduced a vivacious young Quaker,
   And, when he had done it,
   She straightened her bonnet,
And said: "I give thanks to my Maker!"

There is a young lady, called Flynn,
Who thinks fornication a sin;
    But, when she is tight,
    She considers it right,
So everyone fills her with gin!

There was a young lady of Lundy,
Began fresh affairs on a Monday,
    Thus enlarging, each week,
    Her erotic technique,
Whilst chastely abstaining each Sunday.

WFN WATSON

A schoolgirl, who'd reached adolescence,
Wondered what did they mean by pubescence?
    Said the vicar: "A dame
    And a chap ain't the same!"
And he widened her split with the difference!

There was an old monk in Siberia,
Whose existence grew steadily drearier,
    Till he fled from his cell
    With a hell of a yell,
And eloped with the Mother Superior!

There was a old friar named Tuck,
Whose sex life was marred by foul luck;
    His physique grew so fat
    That he could not get at
His poor cock when he wanted a fuck.

There was an old monk of Siberia,
Who fancied the Mother Superior;
   Each time she walked past,
   He'd grab at her vast
And exquisitely rounded posterior!

RON RUBIN

      A parson, who lived in King's Lynn,
      Said he thought fornication a sin,
         Till a girl said: "You fool!"
         Whilst unzipping his tool,
      Bending over and shoving it in!

An impressionable girl from Cape Cod
Had thought babies were fashioned by God;
   It was not the Almighty
   Who hoisted her nightie,
But Roger the lodger, the sod!

There was a young damsel named Baker,
Who was poked in a pew by a Quaker;
   He yelled: "My God, what
   Do you call this – a twat?
Why, the entrance is over an acre!"

The Conquering Lion of Judah,
Offered prayer to the statue of Buddha;
   "Oh, idol," he prayed,
   "May Il Duce be spayed,
And all his descendants be neuter!"

"Oh, Mother! I can't be a nun –
I'm too fond of the pastry cook's son."
   "It's only a crush.
   You must give him the brush!"
"It's too late, Ma, I'm baking his bun!"

There was an old lady from Bonn
Who, when autumn was nearly all gone,
   Bought some really thick knickers
   She showed several vicars,
Who all cried: "Ah! Winter drawers on!"

MELISSA LAWRENCE

A medieval reclusive named Sissons,
Was alarmed by nocturnal emissions;
　　His cell-mate, a sod,
　　Said: "Oh, leave it to God."
And taught him some nifty positions.

A horny old monk of Regina,
Announced: "There is nothing diviner
　Than to sit in one's cell
　And permit one's mind dwell
On the charms of the Virgin's vagina."

A lecherous Bishop of Peoria,
In a state of continual euphoria,
　　So enjoyed having fun
　　With a whore or a nun,
While chanting the Sanctus and Gloria.

There once was a priest of Gibraltar,
Who wrote dirty jokes in his psalter;
　An inhibited nun,
　Who had read every one,
Made a vow to be laid on his altar.

A young curate, just new to the cloth,
Was in no way a sexual sloth;
　　He preached masturbation
　　To the whole congregation,
And was washed down the aisle on the froth.

There was an old monk from Dundee,
Who hung a young nun in a tree;
   He grabbed her fair ass,
   And performed a high mass
That even the Pope came to see.

      There are some things we mustn't expose,
      So we hide them away in our clothes;
         It is shocking to stare
         At what's clearly there,
      Although why this is so Heaven knows!

There was a young choirboy from Devon,
Who was raped in a haystack by seven
   High Anglican priests
   (Lascivious beasts) –
For of such is the kingdom of Heaven.

      Said Fifi: "With bondage, I've found
      That punters will phone and come round,
         To be trussed like a chicken,
         And whipped till they're kicking –"
      Said the Bishop: "That's fun, I'll be bound!"

JOHN SLIM

There was a young curate of Eltham,
Who wouldn't fuck girls, though he felt 'em;
   In lanes he would linger,
   And play at stink-finger,
And scream with delight when he smelt 'em.

Three lustful young ladies of Simms,
Were blessed with such over-size quims,
   The bishop of their diocese
   Got elephantiasis,
For his life wasn't all singing hymns.

      These verses, one can but surmise,
      Weren't intended for innocent eyes;
         Should the Bishop, or Dean,
         Ascertain what they mean,
      They'd be sure to turn pink with surprise!

The priest, a cocksucker named Sheen,
Is delighted his sins are not seen;
   "Though God sees through walls,"
   Says Monsignor "Oh, balls!
This God stuff is simply a screen."

      There was a young girl whose divinity
      Had preserved her in perfect virginity,
         Till a candle, her nemesis,
         Caused parthenogenesis –
      Now she thinks herself one of the Trinity.

There was a young friar of Byhill,
Who clambered to shit on a high hill;
   When the abbot asked: "Was it
   A goodly deposit?"
He said: "*Vox et praeterea nihil*"*

*"*A voice and nothing more.*"

I once had the wife of a Dean,
Seven times while the Dean was out ski'in;
    She remarked with some gaiety:
    "Not bad for the laity,
Though the Bishop once managed thirteen!"

        There was an archbishop in France,
        Who saw a nude woman, by chance;
            The result, I affirm,
            Was emission of sperm
        In the archiepiscopal pants.

There was a young priest from Madrid,
Who looked with lewd eyes at a kid;
    He said, and I quote:
    "I could bugger that goat –
I'll be damned if I don't!" And he did.

        The Bishop of Winchester Junction,
        Found his phallus would no longer function;
            So, in black crepe he wound it,
            Tied a lily around it,
        And solemnly gave it last unction.

There was a young girl in a cast,
Who had an unsavoury past,
    For the neighbourhood pastor
    Tried fucking through plaster,
And his very first fuck was his last.

There was a young angel named Jaylo,
Who, next to his arse, wore his halo;
   When asked its intent,
   He replied, as he bent,
"It sanctifies those who would play low."

      A surly and pessimist Druid,
      A defeatist, if only he knew it,
         Said: "The world's on the skids,
         And I think having kids
      Is a waste of good seminal fluid."

The Reverend Henry Ward Beecher,
Thought a girl a most elegant creature;
   As she laid on her back,
   And, exposing her crack,
Cried: "Fuck that, you old Sunday School teacher!"

      The late Brigham Young was no neuter,
      No faggot, no fairy or fruiter;
         Where ten thousand virgins
         Succumbed to his urgings,
      There now stands the great State of Utah.

There was a young laundress of Lamas,
Who imagined high amorous dramas;
   From the spots she espied,
   Dried and hardened, inside
The pants of the parson's pyjamas!

There was a young parson from Goring,
Who found a knot-hole in the flooring;
   He lined it all round,
   Then laid on the ground,
And declared it was cheaper than whoring.

A frustrated old parson of Lundy,
Fell asleep in his vestry one Sunday;
   He awoke with a scream:
   "What? Another wet dream!
That's what comes of no fucking since Monday."

As an impatient parson from Harwich,
Tried to mount his betrothed in their carriage;
   Said she: "Hold hard, young goose,
   Please employ self-abuse –
And the other we'll try after marriage."

There was a young man from King's Lynn,
Whose cock was the size of a pin;
    Said his girl, with a laugh,
    As she felt for his staff:
"Golly, this won't be much of a sin!"

There was a young whore from Tashkent,
Who performed in an immoral tent:
    Day out and day in,
    She lay writhing in sin,
Giving thanks it was ten months to Lent.

There was an old Bishop from Brest,
Who openly practised incest;
    "My sisters and nieces
    Are all willing pieces,
And don't cost a cent," he confessed.

There was a young curate from Buckingham,
Criticized by the girls for not fucking 'em;
    Said he: "Though my cock
    Is as hard as a rock,
Your cunts are too slack – put a tuck in 'em!"

The Bishop was nobody's fool,
(He'd attended a good public school);
    He took down their breeches,
    And buggered those bitches
With his twelve-inch episcopal tool.

There were three young ladies of Birmingham,
And this is the scandal concerning 'em:
    They lifted the frock,
    And tickled the cock
Of the Bishop engaged in confirming 'em.

        There once was a lady who'd sinned,
        Who said, as her abdomen thinned:
            "By my unsullied honour,
            I'm not a madonna –
        My baby has gone with the wind!"

"I'll admit," said a lady named Starr,
"That a cock's not unlike a cigar;
    But to ordinary people –
    A phallic church-steeple?
That's stretching the matter too far!"

        A hermit frequented oases,
        And thought them the perfect of places;
            Where he prayed and was calm,
            Neath the coolest date palm,
        While the lice on his bollocks ran races.

When Paul the Apostle lay prostrate,
And leisurely fondled his prostate,
    With pride parabolic,
    His most apostolic
Appendage became an apostate.

A sensible lady named Wilde,
Has kept herself quite undefiled,
　　By thinking of Jesus,
　　Contagious diseases,
And the bother of having a child.

There's a randy young dandy named Birch
Who's developed a taste for the church;
　　Any monks, priests or preachers,
　　And alike mouthy creatures
Are the uplifted ends of his search.

The curate is not a bit witty;
When he sings, it's not pleasant or pretty;
   But he does have recourse
   To a cock like a horse,
Entertaining the Ladies' Committee.

JOHN SLIM

   "Posing naked can often be fun,"
   Said the priest with a wink to the nun;
      She replied: "But I'm chaste."
      He said: "Oh, what a waste,
   I've seen worse on page three of the Sun!"

There was a young Jewess named Hannah,
Who sucked off her lover's banana;
   She swore that the cream
   That shot out in a stream,
Tasted better than biblical manna.

   A lecherous priest from Peru,
   Fucked the deacon's young wife in a pew;
      "I'll admit I'm not pious,
      And it's true, I've a bias –
   I just think it diviner to screw."

There's a naughty old vicar of Wadham, he
Is highly enamoured of sodomy;
   Though he's shyly confessed:
   "I like tongue-fucking best –
God bless my soul, isn't it odd of me?"

A bishop, who's had a few drinks,
Observes a young tart as she winks;
 Says the randy old trout:
 "She's about to find out
That a bishopric's not what she thinks!"

JOHN SLIM

A pious young maiden named Finnegan,
Cautioned her beau: "Now you're in again,
 Please time it just right,
 So you'll last through the night –
I most certainly don't wish to sin again!"

An impish young lady of Fife,
Who'd played practical jokes all her life,
 Abandoned her knickers
 One day at the vicar's,
To worry the man and his wife!

JOHN SLIM

A pious old woman named Peak,
Who had taught her vagina to speak,
 Was frequently liable
 To quote from the Bible –
During fucking? Well, barely a squeak!

From the depths of the crypt at St Giles,
Came a scream that resounded for miles;
  Said the vicar: "Good gracious!
  Has Father Ignatius
Forgotten the Bishop has piles?"

Said the curate: "Young Hugh, you are right –
The vicar's a man of great might;
  But his style's out of fashion,
  And he hasn't the passion,
So he can't come six times in one night!"

Mused Hugh: "It was only November,
In the organ loft as I remember;
  He took off his cassock,
  Sat me on a hassock,
And made me shake hands with his member!"

"And, as I shook faster, it grew,
Shooting jism so straight and so true,
  That, from a distant position,
  He achieved full coition –
Shall I ask him to point it at you?"

Years later that young man called Hugh,
Was tossing himself in a pew,
  When, reproached by the vicar,
  He replied: "It's far quicker
Than when I took lessons from you!"

No one could call me a prude,
But I did think it frightfully rude
   Of the vicar's wife, Mabel,
   To jump on the table,
And perform a pas seul in the nude

(Except for the rose in her hair),
And what led to this sorry affair
   Was the man she sat next to
   (I'm afraid over-sexed) who
Had plied her with J&B Rare.*

CYRIL RAY

* *J&B Rare – a delicate blend of Scotch whisky.*

A monk, from a Lincolnshire priory,
Went to see the film "Bridget Jones' Diary";
   The total effect
   Made him somewhat erect,
And his general demeanour more fiery.

        "I'll admit," said the vicar, "One vice:
        A fond memory, naughty but nice;
           I have let my cock
           Lift the organist's frock
        Just the once... no – I tell a lie – twice!"

A young curate's daughter, from Ealing,
Often hung upside down from the ceiling,
   Crying out: "Look here, now, sirs
   Were I wearing trousers –
What you see would be far less revealing!"

TERRY TAPP

        There are numerous jolly old vicars,
        Who'll cavort about wearing silk knickers;
           Exercise, if you will,
           That instills such a thrill,
        It's supposed to be good for their tickers!

To bump off old vicars with tickers
Deemed dodgy, no trick works as quick as
   Simply pursing one's lips
   (Young Miss Hopkins insists)
And confiding: "I'm wearing no knickers!"

There's an orgy tonight at The Manse,
And you must pop along if you've chance;
   There'll be plenty of cock,
   So, yes – don a posh frock,
But there's no need to wear any pants!

Said the Bishop, well-pleased to have scored
With the actress he'd met, while abroad:
   "It seemed to get harder
   In your Lada in Garda
Than at home, on my own, in a Ford!"

JOHN SLIM

There was an old vicar of Eastleigh,
Whose habits were perfectly priestly;
    Till one day in the crypt,
    When his saintliness slipped
And he did something perfectly beastly!

RON RUBIN

Said a priest to a nun: "I'm not clear:
What's a blow-job? Can you tell me, my dear?"
    She said: "Father, indeed,
    Fifteen quid's what you need –
You'll find that's the rate around here."

A Salvation Army lass, Claire,
Was enjoying her first love affair;
    As she climbed into bed,
    She reverently said:
"I wish to be opened by prayer."

Asked what he desired most of all:
"A penis!" said the Pope, named John Paul,
    Cried a Cardinal: "No!
    It is not pronounced so –
But 'appiness if I recall."

A frustrated young priest of Westphalia,
Went out on a wild Bacchanalia;
    He rogered a nun,
    Screwed a friar for fun,
Then the Bishop, in fullest regalia!

The prudish old Bishop of Florence,
Wrote anti-sex pamphlets in torrents,
   Till a choirboy called Billy
   Showed him his wee willy,
And he burnt all his tracts with abhorrence.

     Whenever I wear winklepickers,
     The soft footsteps behind are the vicar's;
       I believe it's my shoes
       That he likes to peruse –
     Or perhaps it's the cut of my knickers!

A Cardinal, living in Rome,
Installed a Greek bath in his home,
    Full of statues, undraped,
   With their bums nicely shaped,
And he loved to toss off in the foam.

     A genteel old lady I knew,
     Was dozing one day in her pew;
       When the Preacher yelled: "Sin!"
       She cried: "Yes! Count me in,
     As soon as the service is through!"

The Bishop of Worcester (so rude!)
Loved to romp with a blonde in the nude;
   If she moaned: "Oh, my Lord!
   With plain screwing I'm bored" –
He'd suggest something equally lewd.

In church, the bride's mother said: "Dear,
Your way to success is quite clear:
   He'll lead, but you'll find,
   If you push from behind,
He'll go any way that you steer!"

       "Given faith," quoth the Vicar of Deneham,
       "From the lusts of the flesh we might wean 'em;
          But the human soul sighs
          For a nice pair of thighs,
       And a little of what lies between 'em."

A lady, quite truly devout,
Once shocked all her friends round about;
   She explained: "Very few
   Have a clue what I'll do
On a gin and a bottle of stout!"

       They say that our parson's young daughter,
       Loved sex like no decent girl oughter;
          But nothing she did
          Stimulated her id
       Like the spanking she got when he caught her.

A naughty young missy's transgression,
Led her straight to a priest in confession;
   While asking for pardon
   She gave him a hard-on
They shared at the end of the session.

JOHN SLIM

A vice most obscure and unsavoury,
Kept the Bishop of Durham in slavery
    Midst terrible howls
    He'd deflower young owls
In his crypt, fitted out as an aviary.

God's plan made a hopeful beginning,
But Man spoilt his chances by sinning;
    We trust that the story
    May end in great glory,
But, at present, the other side's winning!

The imposing cathedral, at Rheims,
Has inspired innumerable wet dreams;
 It looks so like a phallus
 (But bear it no malice),
'Twas the builder's intention it seems.

   Three old deaconesses from Kent,
   Gave up all copulation for Lent;
    This included broom handles,
    Milk bottles and candles,
   And anything else – straight or bent!

There was an old girl from East Sheen,
Who crept into the vestry, unseen;
 She ripped off her knickers,
 Likewise the vicar's,
And said: "How about it, old bean?"

   There was a young choirboy, from Crewe,
   Who declared, as the curate withdrew:
    "Well! The vicar's a prick a
    Substantial lot thicker,
   And several times slicker than you!"

The dark deeds of the Dean of Westminster,
Involved an insatiable spinster;
 To ensure she was clean
 (In spirit, I mean),
He filled up the font first – then rinsed her.

There was a old lady from Twickers,
Who decided to strip at the vicar's;
    When she took off her bra
    He cried: "Please! No, too far!"
So she stopped when she came to her knickers.

KEITH SHEPHERD

The naughty old Bishop of Birmingham,
Used to roger the girls while confirming 'em;
    Amidst roars of applause,
    He would rip off their drawers
And pump his Episcopal sperm in 'em!

An unhappy old Bishop of Fife,
Had a nymphomaniacal wife;
    While he preached to his flock,
    Up the tower (near the clock),
Her keen copulations were rife.

An Anglican vicar from Devon,
Declared: "I have only had seven
   Nice choirboys to date,
   But I'll soon make it eight –
And, shortly thereafter, eleven!"

A crowd-pleasing vicar of Nimms,
Would tickle the choristers' quims;
   Said a middle-aged mezzo:
   "It's nice, but I get so
Confused that I can't sing the hymns!"

CORNELIUS DOYLE

Have you heard of old Father McGrath,
Who screws everything in his path?
   With speed most uncanny,
   He ravished the fanny
Of his granny, bent over the bath!

A vicar from near Brentford Dock,
Has a uniquely adjustable cock;
   A remarkable feature
   Which enables this preacher
To satisfy much of his flock!

Have you heard of the Vicar of Kew,
Who processed with his cassock askew?
   An old spinster named Morgan
   Caught a glimpse of his organ,
And fainted away in her pew!

12.
Said a Nurse to a Doctor in Bed and Other Medical Musings

Said crafty old Doctor McBommon:
"Impotence is becoming too common;
   Pills or oysters and honey?
   A waste of good money –
What works every time's a hot woman!"

      A chap with venereal fear,
      Had intercourse in his wife's ear;
         Said she, "I don't mind,
         Except that I find
      When the telephone rings, I don't hear!"

A pox-ridden lady named Rix,
Was enamoured of sucking large pricks;
   One fellow she took
   Was a doctor called Crook –
Now he's in one hell of a fix!

    There was a young lady from Natchez,
    Who was fully equipped with two snatches;
      She often cried: "Shit!
      I would give either tit
    For a chap with equipment that matches!"

A surgeon reported, in Preston:
"The verdict is anal congestion:
   I found an eight-ball,
   And a sail-maker's awl
Halfway up the commander's intestine!"

    A doctor, by passion deluded,
    Found a wino quite drunk and denuded,
      So, fit as a fiddle,
      And hot for a diddle,
    She tied splints to his penis and screwed it!

If intercourse gives you thrombosis,
While incontinence causes neurosis,
   I'd prefer to expire
   Whilst fulfilling desire
Than live on in a state of psychosis.

An unfortunate lady, named Giles,
Had the ugliest bottom for miles;
   Plastic surgeons took pity
   And made it quite pretty –
Less pimples, all dimples and smiles.

To Sadie the touch of a male meant
An emotional, cardiac ailment;
   An acuteness of breath
   Caused her untimely death
In the course of erotic impalement.

A rosy-cheeked lass, from Dunellen,
Whom the Hoboken sailors called Helen,
   In her efforts to please
   Has spread social disease
From New York to the Straits of Magellan!

When his wife said his kiss never thrilled her,
That his loving no longer fulfilled her,
   He ran up massive bills
   For those little blue pills:
His expenditure damn nearly killed her.

JANET SMITH

An amorous writer of verses,
Was especially enamoured of nurses;
   But he found each advance
   In pursuit of romance
Met only with starchy reverses.

      A lissom psychotic named Jane,
      Once kissed every man on the train;
         Said she: "Please, don't panic,
         I'm just nymphomanic –
      It wouldn't be fun were I sane!"

An industrious young obstetrician,
Conceived his financial position
   To depend upon beauty
   And husbandly duty,
And determined and endless coition.

ISAAC ASIMOV

      The Honorable Winifred Wemyss,
      Saw styli and snakes in her dremyss;
         And these she enjeud
         Until she heard Freud
      Say: "Nothing is quite what it semyss!"

There was a poor fellow, a banker,
Who had buboes, the pox and a chancre;
   He picked up all three
   From a whore in Capri,
And he sent her a postcard to thank her.

A no-nonsense nurse, in Japan,
Lifts the men by their pricks to the pan:
   A trick of ju-jitsu,
   And either it shits you,
Or makes you feel more of a man!

There's an ointment to make willies bigger.
It's a fact, be more tactful, don't snigger;
   You'll be hung like a horse,
   Not a real one, of course,
But a fair match for Roy Rogers' Trigger!

In Memory of dear Dr Nugent,
Whose exploits were somewhat imprudent;
   A notorious old queen,
   You could tell where he'd been
By the smile on the face of each student.

Gratified ladies know when
Viagra's involved, because then...
   Inspection, elation,
   Erection, duration,
Longstanding upstanding. Amen.

JOHN SLIM

There was a old rake called Canute,
Who was troubled by warts on his root;
   He poured acid on these,
   Now, whenever he pees,
He can finger his root like a flute.

There once was an innocent miss,
Who feared she'd conceived from a kiss;
   So, as a precaution,
   She had an abortion,
But nought was forthcoming but piss.

There was a young lady named Prentice,
Who had an affair with a dentist;
   To make the thing easier,
   He used anaesthesia,
And diddled her, non compos mentis.

"The testes are cooler outside,"
Said the Doc to the curious bride,
   "For the semen must not
   Become too fucking hot,
And the bag fans your bum on the ride."

There's a charming young girl of high station
Who has ruined her fine reputation;
   When she said she'd the pox
   From much sucking on cocks –
She should really have called it "fellation".

Said a girl to her friend from Milpitas:
"There's a doctor in town who will treat us
   For feminine ills,
   And hot and cold chills,
Or even abort a young foetus."

Said an ovum one night to a sperm:
"You're a very attractive young germ;
   Come join me, my sweet,
   Let our nuclei meet,
And in nine months we'll both come to term."

An adaptable girl from New York
Was expecting a call from the stork;
   So, with infinite caution,
   She performed an abortion,
With an icepick, a spoon and a fork.

There was a young fellow named Runyan,
Whose pecker developed a bunion;
   When he got an erection,
   This painful infection
Gave off a faint odour of onion.

There was a young priest of Dundee,
Who went into the graveyard to pee;
   He cried: "*Pax vobiscum*,**
   Why doesn't the piss come?
I must have the c-l-a-p!"

**Peace be with you*

An ambitious young man of St Giles,
Who'd walked thousands and thousands of miles,
   From the Cape of Good Hope,
   Just to bugger the Pope,
Found he couldn't – the pontiff had piles.

There once was a randy Parisian,
Who fucked an appendix incision;
   Though the girl of his choice
   Was not keen to rejoice
At his horrible lack of precision.

A medical student named Hetrick,
Is practised in matters obstetric;
   From a glance at the toes
   Of the mother, he knows
If the foetus' balls are symmetric.

There was a young girl of Uttoxeter,
And all the young men shook their cocks at her;
   From one of these cocks
   She contracted the pox,
And she poxed all the cocks in Uttoxeter.

Love letters they no longer write us,
To their homes they so seldom invite us;
   It grieves me to say
   They have learned, with dismay,
We can't cure their vulva pruritus.

     A girl with a sebaceous cyst,
     Came as soon as her pussy was kissed;
       Her lover was gratified
       That she was so satisfied,
     But regretted the fun that he'd missed.

A fellow, who slept with a whore,
Despite condoms got his pecker sore;
   Said he, with chagrin:
   "Selling these is a sin!"
Said the chemist: "Caveat emptor."†

† *Caveat emptor – let the buyer beware.*

     An unfortunate lady named Randall,
     Has the clap such as doctors can't handle;
      So this forlorn young floozie
      With her poor, damaged coosie,
     Must resume her delight with a candle.

A fortunate bounder named Biddle,
Was never hard up for a diddle;
   According to rumour,
   His tool had a tumour,
With a fine row of warts down the middle.

Withdrawal, according to Freud,
Is a habit we ought to avoid;
   If practised each day,
   One's poor balls will decay
To the size of a small adenoid.

A neuropath-virgin named Lynne,
Shouted thus just before she gave in:
   "It isn't the deed,
   Or the fear of the seed,
But that big worm that's shedding its skin!"

Geneology fascinates some.
Said Sharon: "I do think it rum:
   Were it not for a fanny
   Belonging to Granny,
I would never have come from Mum's tum."

JOHN SLIM

There was a young harlot named Schwartz,
Whose cock-pit was studded with warts;
   They tickled so nice,
   She fetched a good price
With the studs at the summer resorts.

An erotic neurotic named Sid,
Got his Ego confused with his Id;
   His errant libido
   Was like a torpedo,
And that's why he done what he did.

Said the doctor: "I trust you won't mope;
You are impotent, so you must cope
   With loss of espousal
   Of randy arousal –
There'll be no hard feelings, I hope!"

JOHN SLIM

      There was a young man from Carmi,
      Who could blink himself off with one eye;
         For a while though, he pined,
         When his organ declined
      And malfunctioned, because of a stye!

Those who resort to coition,
With little, if any, tuition,
   May find, like this verse,
   That it's brief, and what's worse –
Like this verse, may precede obstetrician.

      A disgusting old sod of Golditch,
      Had the clap and the syph and the itch;
         His name was McNabs
         (Yes, he also had crabs),
      What a filthy old son-of-a-bitch.

A dashing young dentist in Kent,
Found in practice, wherever he went,
   Girls only too willing
   To have a good filling:
"Open wide!" stirred their carnal intent.

A surgeon whose home was in Filey,
Chopped the balls off young men rather wryly;
   It left them no choice
   About raising their voice,
And explained why they spoke of him highly.

JOHN SLIM

A canny Scots lass named McFargle,
Without coaxing and such argy-bargle,
   Would suck a man's cock
   Till as hard as a rock,
And then save up the sperm for a gargle.

There was a young girl of Mauritius,
Who declared: "That last fuck was delicious,
   But, the next time you come,
   Please, do so up my bum –
That old wart on your cock looks suspicious."

A poor lad, a promising jockey
Has hung up his spurs, now less cocky;
   "I've got saddle-galls
   On both of my balls."
But the doctor has diagnosed gonococci.

There was a young lady from Hitchin,
Who was scratching herself in the kitchen;
   Her mother said: "Rose,
   It's the crabs, I suppose?"
She said: "Yes! And the buggers are itching!"

      There was a young bounder named Fisk,
      Whose fashion of fucking was brisk;
         His reason was: "If
         The bitch has the syph,
      It's a way of reducing the risk."

One night when you're drunk on Dutch Bols,
Try altering usual roles;
   The backward position
   Is great for coition,
And offers the choice of two holes.

      Coitus with a handy cadaver,
      Is the easiest way you can have 'er;
         Her inanimate state
         Means a chap needn't wait,
      And eliminates all the palaver!

Said a nurse to a doctor, in bed:
"I suggest we play Scrabble instead:
    Your dick's defied six
    Of my life-saving tricks –
I'm pronouncing it clinically dead!"

A far-sighted cad of Carlisle,
Looked at life with a lecherous smile;
    Viagra, as planned,
    Put him much in demand,
For a reason that stuck out a mile!

The enjoyment of sex, although great,
Is in later years said to abate;
   And this may well be so,
   But how would I know?
I'm only a hundred-and-eight!

     A surgeon, of some imprecision,
     Had decided on self-circumcision:
        A slip of the knife –
        "Oh, dear!" said his wife,
     "Our sex life will need some revision."

An anaemic old spinster from Stoke,
Who in favour of chastity spoke,
   By her GP was told:
   "If I may make so bold,
What you need is a bloody good poke!"

     An anxious old fellow, named Duff,
     Said: "Doctor, I'm feeling quite rough.
        I've turned ninety-three,
        And I find I can't pee."
     Said the Doctor: "You've peed quite enough."

JOHN SLIM

In an old people's home the surprise
When Viagra arrived was the size
   Of the grin, ear to ear,
   On every old dear
And the lumps in the old fellows' flies!

JOHN SLIM

There is something about satyriasis,
That arouse psychiatrists' biases;
   But we're both very pleased
   We're in this way diseased
As the damsel who's waiting to try us is!

Pubic hair is put there for a reason
That is evident in the cold season:
   For the balls it's a muff,
   For the rod it's a ruff,
And it keeps the vagina from freezin'.

Whilst undressing a maiden named Sue,
Her seducer observed: "If it's true
   That a nipple a day
   Keeps the doctor away –
Think how healthy you are with these two!"

Young girls of seductive proportions
Should take contraceptive precautions;
   But silly young Ermintrude
   Let one little sperm intrude –
Where is the best place for abortions?

Such a stunning impression Sue made,
When she stripped at the Easter Parade
   The boys of St Paul's,
   To a man burst their balls,
And had to be given First Aid.

At a house of ill-fame in Nevada
Girls complained that their work was much harder,
   Since Viagra's effects
   On the opposite sex
Had redoubled their clientele's ardour.

JANET SMITH

There is a young girl of Kilkenny,
On whose genital parts there are many
   Venereal growths,
   The result of wild oats
Scattered there by a bugger named Benny.

13.
Limericks: Immemorially Lavatorial and Rude, Crude and Lewd

A bather whose clothing was strewed,
By strong winds that had left her quite nude,
   Saw a man come along,
   And, unless I am wrong,
You expected this line to be rude!

      If you find for your verse there's no call,
      And you can't afford paper at all,
         For the poet, true born,
         However forlorn,
      There's always the lavatory wall!

Limericks, from time immemorial,
Have established a proprietorial
   Claim on perversions
   And animadversions
And lines by and large lavatorial.

JOHN SLIM

      At Harvard, a randy old Dean,
      Said: "The funniest jokes are obscene.
         To bowdlerize wit
         Takes the shit out of it –
      And who wants a limerick clean?"

The limerick's callous and crude,
Its morals distressingly lewd;
   It's not worth the reading
   By persons of breeding –
It's designed for us vulgar and rude.

Modern limerick verse is imbued,
With suggestion, invariably crude;
   Your fine rhymes, Mr Lear,
   Are outdated, I fear,
By vocabulary risqué and rude.

Dirty jokes have no future at all;
Their appeal is beginning to pall –
   According to rumour
   For lavatory humour,
The writing is now on the wall.

JOHN SLIM

      The limerick form is so easy,
      It's no trick at all to be breezy;
         But the lines of its wit
         Are oft flavoured with shit,
      Thus arousing the qualms of the queasy.

The limerick packs laughs anatomical,
Into space that is quite economical;
   But the good ones I've seen
   So seldom are clean,
And the clean ones so seldom are comical.

      There was a young lady... tut, tut!
      So you think that you're in for some smut?
         Some five-line crescendo
         Of lewd innuendo?
      Well you're wrong. This is anything but.

ACKNOWLEDGMENTS

The editor and publisher are grateful to the following for permission to publish their limericks for the first time in this collection:

MARK BUMFORD

"An adventurous chap from Bombay" copyright © Mark Bumford 2009.

CAROL ANNE DAVIS

"An erotica writer, called May", "Dildo prices, increasingly steep", "A bored laundry worker from Lyme" and "A randy professor from Splott" copyright © Carol Anne Davis 2009.

CORNELIUS DOYLE

"A crowd-pleasing vicar of Nimms", "The muff-diving champ of St Ives", "My landlady frigs every night", "The bottom of Elspeth McEagle" and "A fastidious schoolman named Grigg" copyright © Cornelius Doyle 2009.

ELIZABETH FERRIS

"The impressive Cerne Abbas giant" copyright © Elizabeth Ferris 2009.

RUPERT HANBURY

"There was a young maid of Madras" copyright © Rupert Hanbury 2009.

GEOFF HARRIS

"A lascivious hussy from Ealing" and "A well endowed nudist, from Ongar" copyright © Geoff Harris 2009.

IAN HERBERT

"A lady – by nature quite dour", "A monk from a Lincolnshire priory", "There was a young lady from Cheam", "A knight at King Arthur's Round table", "A young woman from Berwick-on-Tweed" and "Enrique, a lonely young squirrel" copyright © Ian Herbert 2009.

PAMELA TRUDIE HODGE
"Eileen Backwards, at Paddington Station" copyright © Pamela Trudie Hodge 2009.

REG LYNES
"A lady considered a prude", "A beginner who'd gone with a tart", "A tart who was new to the game", "To bump off old vicars with tickers", "There's a small Bed & Breakfast in Ryde", "A practical joker named Ron", "If for all sorts of seabirds you yearn", "There's an orgy tonight at The Manse", "The dildos have all been marked down", "The first time I met Gypsy Rose", "Her boobs have been fashioned from plastic", "When Molly met Milly in Walmart", "The hen-night magician thought quick", "An elderly tart admits: "Men!"", "When she jumped in the back of the car", "I couldn't have been any greener", "There are numerous jolly old vicars," and "A highwayman, robbing a coach" copyright © Reg Lynes 2009.

GERDA MAYER
"A Pole with a pole in a punt" copyright © Gerda Mayer 2009.

BETTY PAGE
"Little boys will be boys will be boys" copyright © Betty Page 2009.

ELEANOR ROGERS
"A young window-dresser called Kay", "A curvaceous dancer called Anne", "A sultry young damsel from Delhi", "A mademoiselle from Marseilles", "Though we study the birds and the bees" and "An unfulfilled caterer, Kate" copyright © Eleanor Rogers 2009.

ANNE RUSSON
"A saucy greengrocer in Leeds" copyright © Anne Russon 2009.

KEITH SHEPHERD
"A desperate old harpy from Umsk", "There was a young lady from Ware" and "There was an old lady from Twickers" copyright © Keith Shepherd 2009.
JANET SMITH

"Don Juan was an amorous gent", "In the park, where he practised his jogging", "At a house of ill-fame in Nevada", "Caesar thought Cleopatra was peachy", "When his wife said his kiss never thrilled her", "When a feminine itch made her ill", "Although Peeping Tom knew it was wrong", "As a trainee upholsterer, he", "When they named an inflatable vest", "A diminutive person called Willie", "Said the Marquis de Sade: 'I'm inventive'" and "On their honeymoon his bride derided" copyright © Janet Smith 2009.

MIKE SPILLIGAN
"I never have thoughts of another", "We go down to Dog Paddle Creek", "He accepted that both balls were out", "In the Sex Shop, the poor girl's heart sank" and "She thought she was safe in that pool" copyright © Mike Spilligan 2009.

NIGEL STRATTON-DAWES
"An unfaithful old bounder called Reg" copyright © Nigel Stratton-Dawes 2009.

MICHAEL SWAN
"There is a pretty young girl in Ostend" copyright © Michael Swan 2009.

TERRY TAPP
"A lad christened William Winkie" and "A young curate's daughter from Ealing" copyright © Terry Tapp 2009.

NICK TOCZEK
WHERE TO DO IT "Hall, kitchen table, landing, loo", "The sex claims of most men disguise", "She's naked in bed with a wimp", "A wealthy old man from Niagara" and "When he'd died his wife cried as if" copyright © Nick Toczek 2009.

DENNIS WALKER
"There was a young lady named Haste", "Lady C felt her gardener adored her" and "As his passenger stripped in North Wales" copyright © Dennis Walker 2009.

TOM WAYTS
"A well-endowed bounder called Rogers", "Some cocks weigh no more than an

ounce", "If you can't get it up, here's the answer", "Some blokes are incredibly hairy", "Since he fought for his Equity card", "A girl who went in for a swim", "The Doctor's cock's quite hard to see", "If you had a hard-on, she'd clock it", "She could hardly believe her own eyes", "Pert nipples like sweet nectarines", "We enquired about sex around town", "Although she looks fairly aloof", "That sexy posh tart you've just met", "Even though there's not much of a plot", "A twelve-inch vermillion cock?", "Roll up, ladies! Why don't you fill those", "Young Bill is so fond of his willy", "I'm in love with a butternut squash", "I'm in luck, I'm in luck, I'm in luck", "Instead of the usual flunkies", "When the hour strikes midnight o'clock", "'I'll admit,' said the vicar, 'One vice:'", "A curious virgin called Ruth", "When a stand-up comedian tried", "An inflatable cock is the thing", "The last time I met Madame X", "Other passengers started to panic", "In the Sex Shop, Fiona's heart sank", "I went straight round but to no avail", "If one cock's not enough for your kicks", "When she met him, she thought: 'Mmm, bit iffy'", "Here he comes, little cocky Cock Robin", "The Marquis de Sade was a bod", "A handful of reasons the Poles", "His bride said: 'We'll fuck in the dark.'", "The first time I delved in his smalls", "'Talk dirty,' she begged him politely", "An elderly tart admits: 'Men!'", "I've encountered some cocks in my time" and "A well-known TV Chat Show host" copyright © Tom Wayts 2009.

LES WILKIE
"The desirable young Lady Chatterley" and "A lady who lives in Moncrieff" copyright © Les Willkie 2009.

ANN WILKS
"There was a young lady from Wales" copyright © Ann Wilks 2009.
We are also grateful for permission to include the following previously published limericks:

ISAAC ASIMOV
"A forthright young maiden of Ealing", "There was a young man of Belgrade", "'On the beach,' said John sadly, 'There's such'", "An industrious young obstetrician", "There was a young woman of Sydney", "A woman from South Philadelphia", "There was a young man from Poughkeepsie", "A certain young

fellow named Vaughan", "Another young woman named Claire", "'I am just,' moaned a girl from Racine", "An Olympian lecher was Zeus", "A young woman from South Carolina", "A young violinist named Biddle", "A Sultan said sadly: 'One strives'", "'What a shame!' said a winsome young miss", "Said a woman, with open delight:", "In her youth exhibitionist Annie", "A young teacher from far-off Bombay", "Said a man from Mobile, Alabama", "Young Jane was a lollapalooza", "A fellow from Chicopee, Mass", "During sex Mary's moans were harmonic", "How bitter was Joseph's existence", "A luscious young student at Vassar", "There was a young woman named Melanie", "Thanks to sex a young woman named Carol" and "There was an old man from the Nile" copyright © Isaac Asimov, previously published in *Lecherous Limericks* by Isaac Asimov (Panther Books). All efforts to trace the copyright holder were unsuccessful.

JEDEDIAH BARROW

"The Last Ride Together" copyright © Jedediah Barrow, previously published in the *New Statesman* and *Never Rub Bottoms with a Porcupine* (George Allen & Unwin) 1979, and reproduced with the permission of the author.

GERARD BENSON

"There was a young princess, Snow White", copyright © Gerard Benson, previously published in *The Penguin Book of Limericks* compiled and edited by E. O. Parrott (Penguin Books) 1983, and reproduced with the permission of the author.

CYRIL BIBBY

"A musical maiden from Frome" copyright © Cyril Bibby, previously published in *The Art of The Limerick,* by Cyril Bibby (The Research Publishing Co.) 1978. All efforts to trace the copyright holder were unsuccessful.

SHEILA HOPKINS

"A young motorcyclist from Horton" copyright © Sheila Hopkins, previously published in *The Mammoth Book of Limericks,* edited by Glyn Rees (Constable & Robinson) 2008 and reproduced with the permission of the author.

FROM *I'M SORRY I HAVEN'T A CLUE*

"The best way to read Conan Doyle", "When drinking a cup of Earl Grey", "A radical curate from Brent", "I once spent a weekend in Hove", "When Santa gets bored in his grotto", "A Welshman who are some Caerphilly", "At an orgy old Julius Caesar", "I've a small breed of dog called a Scottie", "There's a café in old Milton Keynes", "Whenever I wear winklepickers" and "Posing naked can often be fun" copyright © the individual authors, previously published in *I'm Sorry I Haven't A Clue,* compiled by Jon Naismith (Orion Media) 1998. All attempts to trace the copyright holder/s were unsuccessful.

PETER LUCAS

"There was a young man from East Anstey" and "An old lighthouse-keeper from Orme" copyright © Peter Lucas, previously published in *The Mammoth Book of Limericks*, edited by Glyn Rees (Constable & Robinson) 2008, and reproduced with the permission of the author.

REG LYNES

"I shall nurture my 48D", "'I admit I'm a bit of a tart'", "An aristocratic old Count" and "There are several good reasons why Walter" copyright © Reg Lynes, previously published in *The Mammoth Book of Limericks*, edited by Glyn Rees (Constable & Robinson) 2008, and reproduced with the permission of the author.

E O PARROTT

"There was a young outlaw named Hood", "A couturier, from Haverfordwest", and "A bashful young fellow of Brighton" copyright © E O Parrott, previously published in *The Penguin Book of Limericks* compiled and edited by E O Parrott (Penguin Books) 1983, and reproduced with the permission of Mrs Tricia Parrott.

FROM *THE PENGUIN BOOK OF LIMERICKS*

"One midnight, old D. G. Rossetti", "There was a young girl of Trebarwith", "A gay soccer spectator from Wix", "When the census man called upon Gail", "'Oh, halt!' cried Virginia, 'Enough!'", "A Texan Rhodes Scholar named Ned", "A lass of curvaceous physique", "There was a young lady of Lundy", "There was a young fellow called Shit", "A prostitute living in London", "A slow-footed stockman called Beales", "King Richard, in one of his rages", "There was a young boy, Jack Horner", "A platinum blonde, Goldilocks", "Said old Father William: 'I'm humble', "I once took my girl to Southend", "'Active balls?' said an old man of Stoneham", "There was a young fellow called Crouch", "Undressing a maiden called Sue" and "A naïve young lady of Cork" and "'How much,' sighed the gentle Narcissus", copyright © the individual authors, previously published in *The Penguin Book of Limericks,* compiled and edited by E O Parrott (Penguin Books) 1983. All attempts to trace the copyright holders were unsuccessful.

CYRIL RAY

"No one could call me a prude", "My God, he's an impudent fella", "I'm the victim of vile sabotage", "A gentleman ought to show gratitude", "I do like a nice glass of brandy", "There was a young lady of Kent", "Let me tell you the think that I've thunk –", "I was sitting there, taking my ease", "At last I've seduced the au pair", "I was far from successful with Susie", "The family party grew merrier", "A girl doesn't need to be witty", "On oysters washed down with Frascati", "There's this to be said for Verdicchio", "'With the coffee,' Tom said, 'I insist'", "Girls of Bordeaux, I'm afraid" and "Vodka's the stuff for the Reds – " copyright © Cyril Ray, previously published in *Lickerish Limericks,* by Cyril Ray (JM Dent & Sons Ltd) 1979 and reproduced with the kind permission of Mrs Elizabeth Ray.

RON RUBIN

"A frigid young lady from Gloucester", "My girlfriend who lives down in Dallas is", "A victim of sexual repression", "When a fat striptease dancer debuted", "A bashful young lady of India", "A newly-wed couple called Birch", "A young lad from Auckland called PeeWee", "A fraulein from Alstadt-am-Rhein", "The sex-mad young son of Lord Bicester", "In Eden, the first man, called Adam", "Said cosmonaut Katie to Pete:", "Whilst cruising the cosmos, McCavity", "There was a young lady of Burma", "Nostalgic in old Aberystwyth", "There once was a great prima donna", "There was an old monk of Siberia", "There was an old Welshman, called Morgan", "'I'm glad pigs can't fly,' said young Sellers", "There was an old drunkard of Devon", "There was a young waiter, called Fritz", "There was a young lady called Sue", "In a hardware store, sex-mad young Stu", "There was a trombonist, called Grange", "There was a young lady called Kate", "A vigilant watchdog called Mary", "Gentlemen, dining in Bude", "'We've a new French chanteuse,' grumbled Lars", "A rakish young toff, name of Hal", "There was an old fellow called Frank", "A train-spotting couple of Harwich", "There was an old fellow of Harrow", "A kinky old cowboy, called Marriott", "Said a pious young bride of Toledo", "A well-travelled floozie of Ealing", "A buxom young dancer called Cleo", "There was a plump lass, called Louisa", "There was an old vicar of Eastleigh", "Said a lonely old man called Le Mesurier", "There was an old cockney called Warner", "There was an old German, called Rosen", "There was a young girl of Uttoxeter", "There was an old codger of Poole", "There was an old Greek God called Zeus", "A guitarist by name of Renato", "Chopin – let's just call him Fred –", "A lady guitarist of Bude", "An Athenian singer called Nina", and "'Do you know,' asked a punter called Dai" copyright © Ron Rubin, previously published variously in *Out on a Limerick, How to be Tremendously Tuned in to Opera, A Medley of Musical Limericks, Forum, Mayfair,* and reproduced with the permission of the author.

STANLEY J SHARPLESS
"Widow (conscious that time's on the wing)", "'Monsieur Gauguin? E's gone to Tahiti'" and "There was a young lady… tut, tut!" copyright © Stanley J. Sharpless, previously published in *The Penguin Book of Limericks*, compiled and edited by E O Parrott (Penguin Books) 1983, and reproduced with the permission of Campbell Thomson & McLaughlin Ltd.

JOHN SLIM
"An anxious young fellow named Sean", "A poet whose verses inclined", "In church, the bride's mother said: 'Dear'", "There's a fellow in Abergavenny", "She has marks on her knees which she shows", "A computer buff's ancient jalopy", "There's a bimbo who's anxious to score", "She cried: 'You're a filthy old fart'", "Said a nurse to a doctor, in bed:", "The risks that he took were quite minimal", "A lady, quite truly devout", "A pretty young harlot, in court", "Don't ever do that again!", "A lusty young lady, named Gwen", "The bride told the best man: 'We'll share'", "There's a fellow whose cocktail quips", "She yelled at her husband: 'You prat!'", "When people could not understand", "There was a young lady, named Glad", "Dear Doctor, I need your advice", "When supping some vin ordinaire",

"Said Wendy the waitress: 'I try'", "A gentleman said: 'When I doff'", "A bonny young Scots laddie, built", "Said Bert: 'Let's be wheelbarrow-lovers'", "Said a priest to a nun: 'I'm not clear:'", "A bit of a nuisance named Liam", "Old Nora still knows how to please", "A gratified lassie, amazed", "A brassy young lass attracts stares", "Said Brenda, a bit of a dish:", "Geoff and old Flo, who was flirty", "When ladies were laid in Kincaid", "She exclaimed, while replacing the truss", "A far-sighted cad of Carlisle", "There was a young man of Ancona", "A bride in Bangkok got a shock:", "An eager young man, from Belize", "When Tom lost his dad in Biarritz", "A long-plonkered fellow called Keith", "Said a baffled young bimbo of Brent:", "Said an innocent lad from Caerphilly", "There is a young fellow from Crick", "Gasped a golfer in old Donegal:", "In the street, a big lady from Fareham", "Said the lad: 'Have you heard of Flat Lick?'", "A floosie from Frankfurt's grown fond", "A wistful young lady, in Garda", "A languid young fellow, from Goole", "She's known to be prone to invite", "Said a lady who'd strayed in Kincaid", "A lady of Leck is lamenting", "A kindly young lady of Lille", "There was a young lady of Lydd", "A naughty young nympho, in Norway", "Said a goose-pimpled stripper of Preston:", "A lecher, around Ringaskiddy", "A lovely young thing, of St Kitts", "Though fellows have frequently found", "When a man in a van (it's a camper)", "A trucker in old Tennessee", "Tina's tennis has earned her renown", "A one-legged workman from Wick", "A male ballet dancer wears gear", "Curvaceous young ladies are full", "'I'm dreadfully sorry!' Fred cried", "A randy bisexual punk", "A dashing young dentist in Kent", "Those who resort to coition", "Said a Parisian actor called Alec", "Possessive wife, mother of two", "The ghost of a long-dead old Dean", "A fencing contractor did well", "A lovely young Swedish au pair", "Said Fred: 'I'd find sex more appealing'", "On the hearthrug in front of the Baxi", "Said a pensive young thing in Valletta", "Said Jack: 'Do you think we should sort of'", "A mini-dinked fellow called Trevor", "A hard-up young callgirl was brash", "A hooker who's also a cook", "A punter felt rather a prat", "Said the tart: 'From the start, to be blunt'", "No danger you might drop a clanger", "Two gardeners, Plantem and Pickem", "The ageing of man, grumbles Wendy", "A lap-dancing club is a place", "A satisfied lady called Bridget", "That push-it-in-double chap (Kent)", "Said Brenda, a bit of a dish:" and other limericks copyright © John Slim, previously published variously in *Rotten Haystacks, Rather Rottener, Multiple Buttocks,* and *Verse Places,* and reproduced with the permission of the author.

JANET SMITH

"James Bond is an agent I've heard" copyright © Janet Smith, previously published in *The Mammoth Book of Limericks*, edited by Glyn Rees (Constable & Robinson) 2008, and reproduced with the permission of the author.

MIKE SPILLIGAN

"A keeper who's fucked quite a few", "She sent me a text on my phone:", and "She jumped in the car and we sped" copyright © Mike Spilligan, previously published in *Forty Naughties* by Mike Spilligan (Shelf Life) 2001, and reproduced with the permission of the author

TOM WAYTS

"There's an ointment that makes willies bigger", "A young Spaniard who's hung like a horse", "A bit of a wanker named Willy", "A naturist rambler named Ron", "Prince Charming was worried to bits", "Ex-telephonist Gladys, I'm told", "A talented painter called Duff", "A young lady whose breasts were quite wee", "A golfer who drives with some force", "A gorilla that lives in the Zoo", "A barrel of lard known as Lyn", "A bat and a bat in a cave", "I may look fairly old and sedate", "There was a young girl from Penzance", "A keen lassie who has to have cock", "A Hollywood star named De Niro", "A friend has an end to his member", "A whore for a bit of a joke", "A well-endowed chap with a cock", "A geneticist living in Rheims", "Mickey's is bigger than Dickie's", "A young lass with a prize-winning bum", "There's a grouchy old farmer near Neath", "A small Bed & Breakfast in Crete", and "A chap on a diet of fruit" previously published in *The Mammoth Book of Limericks*, edited by Glyn Rees (Constable & Robinson) 2008, and reproduced with the permission of the author. Every effort has been made to trace copyright holders. We would be grateful to hear from any copyright holders not acknowledged here.

Special thanks, for a variety of good reasons, are due to:
Gerard Benson, Margaret Brace, Cirencester Lending Library, Pete Duncan, Sheila Hopkins, Gray Jolliffe, Ralph "Rhymer" Jordan (Canfield, Ohio cellar collection), Reg Lynes, Septimus Maggs (Duntisbourne Rous, Gloucestershire attic archive), Monmouth Lending Library, The National Library of Wales, Duncan Proudfoot, Mrs Elizabeth Ray, Frank Richards and Ron Rubin.